JOSEP CARNER · NABÍ

Josep Carner
Nabí

Translated from Catalan by J. L. Gili

Catalan text edited by Jaume Coll
Preface by Jonathan Gili
Introduction by Arthur Terry

ANVIL PRESS POETRY

Published in 2001
by Anvil Press Poetry Ltd
Neptune House   70 Royal Hill   London SE10 8RF

Catalan text of *Nabí* copyright © Hereus de Josep Carner 1998
1998 edition of *Nabí* copyright © Edicions 62, Barcelona 1998
(Edited by Jaume Coll)

Translation copyright © J.F., M.L. and K.M. Gili 2001
Preface copyright © Jonathan Gili 2001
Introduction copyright © Arthur Terry 2001

This book is published with financial assistance
from The Arts Council of England

The publisher is grateful to the copyright holders for
permission to reprint the Catalan text of *Nabí*
and to the Institució de les Lletres Catalanes, Barcelona,
for their support of this publication

Designed and set in Monotype Walbaum by Anvil
Printed and bound in England
by Cromwell Press, Trowbridge, Wiltshire

ISBN 0 85646 330 2

A catalogue record for this book
is available from the British Library

Contents

A Note on the Text

THE CATALAN TEXT of *Nabí* given here is that established by Jaume Coll in his authoritative critical edition, published by Edicions 62/Empúries, Barcelona in 1998. This appeared a few months after the death of Joan Gili.

Jaume Coll's edition of *Nabí* takes into account the three editions directly overseen by Josep Carner – Mexico D.F., 1940 (a fine Castilian version by Carner himself), Buenos Aires, 1941 and Barcelona, 1957 – in the light of the discovery, in 1995, of the printers' proofs from 1938 of an edition scheduled for 1939, publication of which was aborted by the outcome of the Spanish Civil War.

Coll's edition gives both formal and substantial variants with respect to the last text approved by Carner for his major compilation (*Poesia*, 1957), an edition which suffered from proof-reading flaws. The main corrections are: 'pau' for 'nau' at III.67 (p. 50), which Joan Gili had corrected for himself; lower-case initials for 'déu' at VII.193 and 195 (p. 90); a substantial correction in VI.129 (p. 74), where Joan Gili's version has been adjusted; and the restoration of the missing line, not available to Joan Gili, at X.78 ('Ans no passeu del món, hi haurà una meravella:'). Here a literal version has been added in square brackets (p. 117).

As in Jaume Coll's edition, new stanzas or verse paragraphs in the Catalan text are indented so that there is no ambiguity at the foot of a page.

We are grateful to Jaume Coll and Alan Yates for their invaluable assistance in preparing the text for this bilingual edition.

THE PUBLISHER

Foreword

LEXICALLY RICH and written in a variety of metres, *Nabí* makes the task of the translator particularly difficult. By adhering to a strict faithfulness to the text and to the feeling of the pulse of the rhythm, I hope that the translation will 'sing' in its new garb in a way that the English reader may find pleasing.

I would like to thank the heirs of Josep Carner for their permission to translate, and to Albert Manent for being the intermediary. My thanks to my wife, Elizabeth, are in a different dimension: for her encouragement right through, for her sensitive reading of the text next to the original, for saving me from omissions or awkward lines, and for the hours of enjoyment we have had working together. Similarly, to our son Jonathan, on whose good taste and judgement I always rely, for his careful reading of the translation and for his valuable suggestions, these words apply: great thanks.

J. L. GILI
Oxford, 1998

Acknowledgements

MY TASK of bringing Joan's last translation to readers of English has been an absorbing one. I would like to express my heartfelt gratitude for the unfailing encouragement and help given me, in a time of great sorrow, by our children, Jonathan, Martin and Katherine. I am deeply indebted to Arthur Terry for his illuminating introduction, and to Alan Yates for his sympathetic and practical support. I greatly appreciate the friendly interest and advice of Albert Manent, Francesc Parcerisas and Jaume Coll. To Paul Binding and others I owe much for suggesting the publisher of this elegant volume.

ELIZABETH GILI
Oxford, 2001

Preface

THE TRANSLATOR, publisher, antiquarian bookseller and scholar J. L. Gili died in Oxford on May 6th 1998, aged 91. He had lived in England for the last sixty-four years of his life but was born and brought up a Catalan and always thought of himself as having two home towns – Oxford and Barcelona. Though he adopted the name John on his naturalization in 1948, he was known to his family and friends by his Catalan name, Joan. When written rather than spoken, this could cause confusion.

He came from a dynasty of publishers in Barcelona. His grandfather, father and uncle all had their own imprints. His father's, the Editorial Lluís Gili, was founded in 1907, the year Joan was born. It specialized in religious books and only ever produced one best-seller – a cookery book. *Sabores*, written by Joan's mother, was for many years the mainstay of the Spanish bourgeois kitchen. One of his sisters became a Carmelite nun, but he himself was not a believer. He felt stifled by the Victorian values that permeated middle-class Barcelona society.

He was a child when he first met Josep Carner. His father published Carner's *Les monjoies* in 1912 when Joan was five years old, and the poet was a frequent visitor to the Gili office – there was even a table kept for him to work at. But it wasn't until Joan started working for his father – first packing books, later designing them – that they became close. It was Joan who was responsible for preparing the publication of *El veire encantat* (1933) and *Auques i ventalls* (1935). He found that they shared a passion for English literature. They talked about it while reading proofs in the office, they talked about it over dinner. Carner was already an accomplished translator, who had produced Catalan versions of *Robinson Crusoe*, *Alice in Wonderland*, *The Pickwick Papers* and three of Shakespeare's comedies. Joan himself was particularly fond of the English short story, about which he wrote regularly in *La Publicitat*, whose literary editor, the poet J. V. Foix, was married to his sister Victòria. Through Foix he got to know other members of Barcelona's lively literary and artistic world, such as the painter Joan Miró.

Joan Gili's own interest in translation had been stimulated when his father asked him to assist Canon Josep M. Llovera on the Catalan version of St Augustine's *Confessions*. The Canon was also working on a verse translation of Homer's *Iliad*, and Joan was able to see the creative discipline this demanded. He used to refer to his work with Llovera as his 'university education'.

One day he read an article in *The Bookman* that led to a correspondence with its author, C. Henry Warren, a well-known writer about the countryside. When Warren invited him to visit England in 1933, he jumped at the opportunity – but it was only Carner's approval and support that persuaded his father to allow him to go. He fell in love with this country, and the freedom he found here; and in October 1934 returned for good. The Spanish Civil War and the Second World War intervened, and he was not to see his family again for thirteen years.

With Henry Warren he opened the Dolphin Bookshop in Cecil Court, off Charing Cross Road in London. Its name combined two references, to the great printer Aldus Manutius, whose emblem was a dolphin, and to the Mediterranean, where during the Middle Ages it was said that no fish dared show its back unless it had the Catalan flag painted on it.

At first they sold English as well as Spanish books, but it was the Spanish books that made money. He bought out Warren and sold the English stock to Harold Edwards, his neighbour in Cecil Court. The nature of the business was radically altered through a chance encounter in the White Mountains of New Hampshire. Elizabeth McPherson – later to become his wife – met a woman there who told her about a friend who had inherited the bulk of the library built up by the distinguished French Hispanist Raymond Foulché-Delbosc, and was looking for a bookseller she could trust. 'I know the very person,' said Elizabeth.

A railway wagon had to be hired to transport the eight tons of books from Paris to London. Overnight, Joan Gili had become an antiquarian bookseller as well.

The Dolphin Bookshop became the first in Britain to specialize in Spanish and Latin American books and manuscripts. Over the years he built up two important collections – one of material relating to the 18th-century War of Spanish Succession and one of Catalan manuscripts from 911 to 1850 – that are now in the Houghton Library at Harvard.

He started his distinguished series of Hispanic publications in 1938. As well as textbooks and literary studies, there were books (many of them with new English translations) by Miguel de Unamuno, Luis Cernuda, and the Nobel prize-winners Juan Ramón Jiménez and Pablo Neruda. In 1939, he and Stephen Spender translated Rafael M. Nadal's selection of his friend Federico García Lorca's poems, which was one of the first books to introduce Lorca's writing to an English-speaking audience. In 1960 Penguin Books asked him to make new prose translations of Lorca's poems; this bilingual edition was a significant influence on several generations of poets and teenagers.

It was in 1962, when Josep Carner was being proposed for the Nobel Prize, that the two old friends met again. Joan, who wanted to help make his work better-known to an international audience, published a bilingual selection of his poems. Pearse Hutchinson made the translations with help both from Joan and from the anglophile Catalan poet Marià Manent. The entire Gili family drove to Brussels to deliver the first copy to Carner, who was living there in voluntary exile from Franco's Spain. He and his Belgian wife, Émilie Noulet, took us out to supper in a restaurant where we discovered that there are at least twenty-three ways of cooking *moules*, and learnt how to eat *moules à la marinière* without a spoon. Carner was delighted with the book and wrote to say that when he had shown it to friends at the University, their jaws had dropped at the elegance of Joan's typography. 'You are a true *arbiter elegantiarum*,' he said.

The idea for the Dolphin Book Company's most influential publication came from an encounter with Professor William Entwistle. Joan asked him why Catalan was not included in the Oxford syllabus. 'There's no grammar available,' said Entwistle. 'But if you write one, I'll put it in the curriculum.' The result was Joan's *Introductory Catalan Grammar* – the first of its kind, originally published in 1943, when Catalan was banned by Franco's fascists, and still in print today.

Joan used his scholarship to edit the texts he published, and his stylish typographical sense to design all the Dolphin books and catalogues. After Lorca, he helped introduce Catalan poetry to the English-speaking public with his translations of Carles Riba (*Poems*, 1964; *Tankas of the Four Seasons*, 1991; *Savage Heart*, 1993; *Bierville Elegies*, 1995), Salvador Espriu (*Forms and Words*, 1980) and now Josep Carner's *Nabí*.

Riba, who became a close friend, had dedicated the third of his *Elegies de Bierville* to Joan and Elizabeth after staying with them during a visit to London with his wife in 1939:

> . . . so many images and of such
> ah! unthought-of sense have altered for me and are
>   contained
> in the warmth of the two young lovers
> who at the heart of the immense smoky city opened to us
> their paradise full of light, voluptuousness and risk.

Joan had included translations of eight of the *Tankas* in his 1964 selection of poems, and they were set to music the following year by his old friend Alan Rawsthorne. Rawsthorne, Henry Warren and the conductor Harry Blech, together with their patron Helen Gaskell, were his first English friends, and they used to ring each other up every Christmas Day until the end of their lives.

During the War, as a registered alien in London, he was not allowed to help with the war effort, not even to fire-fight. Now married, he decided to move the Dolphin Bookshop away from the bombs to Oxford, to a studio in Park Town that later belonged to the flamboyant purple-waistcoated artist Hector Whistler. There the new baby co-existed happily with the books. The pram was kept in the poetry section, where the eminent lexicographer Dr Onions was once found kneeling on the floor, barking at the infant Jonathan Francesc (now a documentary film director).

By the end of the War they had moved to a Victorian mansion in Fyfield Road, where two more children were born: Martin Lluís (who later took over and still runs the modern side of the book business) and Katherine Montserrat (now a sculptor working in forged steel). The books expanded to fill two floors.

There were only two Catalan families living in Oxford: the Gilis and the Truetas. The celebrated Dr Josep Trueta (first Nuffield Professor of Orthopaedic Surgery and recently the subject of a Spanish postage stamp) and his wife Amèlia became close friends. They kept alive each other's feeling for Catalonia, always talking in an entertaining mélange of the two languages. In 1954, the Catalan nationalist Josep Maria Batista i Roca conceived the idea of an Anglo-Catalan Society, of which Josep Trueta and Joan Gili were founding members and Joan was later President. He became known as the 'unofficial consul of the Catalans in Britain' and was honoured by the Catalan government with the Creu de Sant Jordi for his role in heightening awareness of Catalan literature. King Juan Carlos made him a Comendador de la Orden de Isabel La Católica. His honorary MA from Oxford University, and his attachment to Exeter College, gave him particular pleasure as one who had not had a university education.

For him, work and home were indissoluble. He never retired, and was finalizing corrections to his translation of Josep Carner's *Nabí* when he was struck down by the final stages of cancer. At the age of ninety he was still playing tennis every Saturday. He was always a distinguished figure, with a handsome mane of thick white hair, and he used a safety razor to the end of his life, occasionally changing the brand of shaving cream 'to surprise my beard'.

On his first evening in England, at a dinner party given by Helen Gaskell, he'd met a strikingly beautiful philosophy student with an exotic background. Elizabeth McPherson was born in Hong Kong to a missionary father and an artist mother, and she had spent the first twelve years of her life in China. They didn't take to each other at all.

By the time they decided to marry in 1938, she had graduated with a First from London University and a Henry Fellowship to Yale, but she never seemed to regret abandoning her own career to look after her husband and family. She translated her mother-in-law's cookery book under the title *Tia Victoria's Spanish Kitchen*, and her sumptuous lunches educated the palates of academics and undergraduates alike – though it was Joan who always stepped in to cook the *paella*.

After the wedding, Joan was surprised to learn that Elizabeth had a previous engagement for the weekend, and that he was not invited. 'I let her go,' he said. 'My technique worked – she never left again.'

JONATHAN GILI

Introduction

JOSEP CARNER (1884–1970) was one of the leading members of a brilliant generation of Catalan poets whose work extends from the early years of the century to the aftermath of the Civil War. His early work, with its emphasis on intelligence, good sense and elegance, set a standard for younger poets at a time when the Catalan language itself was at a crucial stage of development. This development had much to do with the official sponsorship of the arts under the presidency of Prat de la Riba (1913–17), but which had begun much earlier, in 1906, with the publication of Prat's own manifesto, *La nacionalitat catalana* (Catalan Nationality) and the first International Congress of the Catalan Language.

After Prat's death in 1917, however, this harmonious situation began to unravel, and in 1921 Carner entered the Consular Service, a decision which was to take him to Geneva, Beirut, Costa Rica, Mexico, and finally to Brussels, where he spent the last twenty-five years of his life. Though he continued to publish in various countries, critical opinion tended to focus on his earlier work, to the detriment of his new poems, many of which showed a deeper sense of compassion and a tendency to speculate on metaphysical questions which go far beyond anything he had achieved before. Above all, perhaps, he seems to have learnt how to use his talent for acute observation as the basis for a new kind of realism in which the moral comment is carried into the details of the poem. This in itself is a sign of the increasing moral complexity of the later poems; even so, the publication of his long poem *Nabí* in 1941[1] must have come as a surprise to even his most dedicated readers, who were accustomed

---

[1] This first edition was published in Buenos Aires. In 1947, a clandestine edition appeared in Barcelona, dated 1938 to escape Franco's censorship.

to regard him as a master of the shorter forms, notably the sonnet and the traditional ballad.

In *Nabí*, one of the three or four best modern Catalan poems of some length, Carner uses the biblical story of Jonah as a means of focusing some of his deepest preoccupations. Its narrative skill and richness of vocabulary alone would make the poem outstanding; what gives it its real stature, however, is the way in which the alternating voices of faith and doubt are made to coincide, with dramatic inevitability, in the concluding vision of hope:

> '. . . For, excepting God, all is transient.
> Who would ever speak of his own eternal radiances
> in a foreign tongue
> and with stuttering lips?
> Farewell, though, to clawing punishment and avarice!
> To die to be born again, clear delight!
> The rebellious man will become love itself.
> For you'll exceed the justice of the Father,
> O maternal purity
> of curd, apples and honey!'

Carner himself once described the theme of the poem as the 'sweet, ironical teaching of forgiveness', and this suggests very clearly where the main thrust of the sequence lies. As for the irony, this comes out most of all in Jonah's self-delusions and in his difficult progress towards a final truth. And, since most of the poem is spoken by Jonah himself, the reader is directly implicated in his personal drama.

The poem is divided into ten cantos, four of which – III, IV, VII and VIII – correspond closely to the biblical text. The others are mostly an invention of Carner's, and it is here that the complexities begin. The first, for example, opens with God's summons to Jonah, which Jonah then makes excuses for avoiding. At the same time, his conscience continues to trouble him – is there really a way of escaping from God? –

and this leads him to accuse God of weakness and finally to insult him:

> Neither Your threats frighten nor Your comfort revives,
> and You appear less resolute,
> like one that wanting to sell a rug
> brings down the price . . .

All this time God has remained silent; in other words, Jonah has been dictating his own text to what he conceives to be God's voice — a voice he would prefer to be one of pure vengeance. God, of course, knows better than this: after the storm and the near-shipwreck, he preserves Jonah in the belly of the great fish and compels him to recognize His power:

> 'God plays. God flings us far, but never away.
> With even voice I sing His name,
> blind, doubled up, as if waiting for a new life
> within the sepulchral tomb. . . .'

So Jonah is reborn, and Canto V begins with a superb evocation of the world to which he is now returned with a sense of exultation. However, he is interrupted by the Voice of God, commanding him once again to go to Nineveh. At this, the delights of nature vanish, and he undertakes the difficult journey which he scarcely survives. Before entering the city, he encounters an old woman — a former priestess of the Dawn — who opposes her vision of ephemeral beauty to Jonah's certitude and makes him wonder, for the first time, whether he is interpreting God correctly. In Cantos VII and VIII, Carner follows the original almost literally, expanding it with touches of vivid detail, but retaining its basic sense. Thus, the king and people of Nineveh listen to Jonah's anathema and, much to his displeasure, are converted. At this point, his dissatisfaction with God surfaces once again:

> I said: "Why have You again shown compassion,
> Jehovah, embracing the wicked
> as You would embrace a new-born? . . ."

Above all, he feels his powers of prophecy have been under-
mined:

> ". . . Who is going to believe me now
> if You let run free those whom You have pursued!
> I felt that You were talking to me face to face,
> and today You turn away from me."

If, as has been said, the original Book of Jonah is a tale of the
education of a prophet, Jonah's education, as Carner presents
it, is still far from complete. Even Ninevites can be pitied by
God, who, the story subversively begins to suggest, might
have wider sympathies than was assumed by a prophet only
interested in relaying the word of a wrathful tribal god. And
so God plays His final trick: the example of the gourd. This
is taken more or less literally from the biblical account: God
makes a gourd grow up overnight to give Jonah more protec-
tion, but then destroys it through sun and wind. Jonah is
indignant and only wishes to die, but God speaks in the form
of a question:

> "You grieve for a little foliage; yet you had
> no part in planting it or making it grow;
> it was a gift of the night air,
> and a morning dew took it away.
> And to Me, who makes and tends all born things,
> should not Nineveh, the three days' city, concern Me;
> aa city with a hundred and twenty thousand children
>   ignorant
> of which is their left or right hand,
> and with numberless sheep-pens
> and great herds of cattle?"

The Book of Jonah ends here, with no response on the part of
Jonah. Carner, on the other hand, makes this passage lead
into what, in many ways, is the climax of the whole poem:

> 'And as Jehovah finished I realized
> that He had not spoken from a clear patch of sky,

but from within myself who had offended Him.
In our soul, where no one perceives Him,
God lives in over a hundred chambers;
and man lies on the threshold of His house
like a servant, like a dog.'

This means that Jonah has not only ceased to complain but that his way of imagining God has become more complex, as has his attitude towards himself. From now on, these images will form part of his mental resources, thereby weakening his older images, though, since he is human, the latter may not disappear entirely. There is an example of this in Canto IX, where Jonah, in a dream, hears a voice 'with an affected Greek accent' (a devil? a representative of Greek rationality?) which denies the existence of God. In the end, Jonah kills the man – if that is what he is – by throwing him over a cliff, thinking that he is avenging his God. Knowing the rest of the poem, we realize that he is mistaken, that he is merely reverting to his former 'wild' self. And this is confirmed by what follows: far from feeling triumph, Jonah experiences shame and a sense of abandonment. But then God speaks for the last time, and his Voice is one of forgiveness and compassion, as Jonah finally recognizes:

'Then, as though drowned in a deeper gully
than my victim, hesitantly I raised my head,
and on seeing written in the starry sky
a clear promise of compassion,
crawling I worshipped His name.'

This is the point towards which the whole poem has been working: the true God, though intolerant of false religions, is a God of forgiveness, not of vengeance. And in the final canto, Jonah, now approaching death, acts as a true prophet by announcing the coming of Christ and at the same time sees himself as one of a line which stretches back through Abraham and Noah to Adam himself.

By retelling the story of Jonah, and by adding his own interpretation, Carner has not only re-created an ancient biblical tale for modern readers, but has provided a supreme example of his art at its fullest stretch. Though it is essentially a Christian poem, it is scathing about the effects of religious perversion, and in the widest sense is a poem about the limits of rationality. But above all it is a triumph of language, of a language which Carner did as much as anyone to establish as a vehicle for serious poetry and which secures *Nabí* a place among the masterpieces of modern European poetry.

As I hope will be clear from my quotations, Joan Gili's translation is itself a minor masterpiece, the result of many years' experience of translating other poems and of studying Carner's original. Few translators could have matched the richness of Carner's vocabulary or have reproduced so accurately the actual rhythms of his poem. In short, he has created a major poem in English for which there is no exact parallel in our language and provided yet another instance of the scope and vitality of modern Catalan poetry.

ARTHUR TERRY

Nabí

*El mot hebreu emprat per a significar «profeta»
és* nabí, *això és, portantveu o torsimany de Déu;
però en l'Escriptura – reconeix Baruch Spinoza en
el seu* Tractatus Theologico-Politicus – *la seva sig-
nificació es contreu a torsimany de Déu.*

The Hebrew word used to signify 'prophet' is *nabí*, that is to say, spokesperson or interpreter of God, but in the Scriptures — as Baruch Spinoza recognizes in his *Tractatus Theologico-Politicus* — its meaning is simply interpreter of God.

I

Al primer traspuntar d'un ventós solixent
d'alta cella vermella,
al jaç de ginesteres es mou espessament
Jonàs, sota el fibló d'un manament:
— Vés a l'esclat de Nínive, trasbalsa cada orella,
retruny per la ciutat:
« Jo, Iahvè, sé la vostra malvestat:
de tant de pes la meva destra s'ha cansat» —.

Jonàs, fill d'Amittai, mal obeïa. Encara
tèrbol, ranquejador,
guerxava els dits per no plegar la vara
ni despenjar el sarró.

— No — diu Jonàs —.
Aquest cop, oh Iahvè, prou seria endebades.
Em sento las
de visions i caminades.
No moguis amb més pressa romboll en mes diades.
¿Qui faria cabal de mi?
Ja contra la percinta del cel no em sé tenir
per invocar ni maleir.
Miolo com l'ocell de nit, car la vellesa
ma veu escanyolí.

Ja no só fer, sinó minvat per la tristesa.

Que em vagui, al caire de les acaballes,
de fer-me perdedor.
Com d'altres. Com qui mai no et sent en cap remor.
Com aquell amb qui calles.
Que igual em sigui l'un i l'altre dia,
un solc i un altre solc dels sementers.

I

At the break of a windswept rising sun,
high red brow on the horizon,
Jonah stirs heavily on his bed of broom branches,
stung by an imperious command:
'Go unto glittering Nineveh, storm every ear,
boom all over the town:
"I, Jehovah, know your evil ways:
my right hand is weary with their weight."'

Jonah, son of Amittai, recalcitrant
and still confused, lingers
twiddling his thumbs, not picking up his staff
or taking down his sack.

'No', said Jonah,
'this time, O Jehovah, it would be in vain.
I'm tired
of visions and journeys.
Do not hasten now the whirling of my days.
Who would listen to me?
I can no longer stand up against the sky
to invoke or curse.
I screech like the night bird,
for my voice has shrivelled with old age.

'I'm no longer fierce, just weakened by sadness.

'Let me, at the end of my days,
slip away quietly.
As others have done. Like one deaf to Your whisper.
Like one with whom You remain silent.
Let my days be evenly balanced
like furrows in a ploughed field.

Xaruc, el terrissaire cap motlle no canvia;
la vella matinera fa d'esma son endreç.
Fes-me negat per a la teva esgarrifança
com qui, son pa començant de menjar,
no té cap pensament que el destriï del pa,
com qui de tan somort ja no sent enyorança,
com qui no sap què sigui mai recança
del que jamai vindrà.

Un temps, Iahvè, no fou la meva nit opresa
ni jo tirat de sobte a cada estrany camí.
Tenia el meu ofici: cap a la tasca apresa
em decantava l'oratjol cada matí.
Vivia en mon poblet, ran de boscatge;
i m'hi gruava el companatge
pensant si compraria la vinya del coster.
En havent-hi bastit cercaria muller
i, en la nit gomboldat, plantaria llinatge.
(És bo que l'home tingui un lloc
i que, quan torni de la treballada,
s'assegui en el llindar i esguardi l'estelada,
i que la dona, que s'atansa a poc a poc,
digui, feixuga: «D'haver nat estic pagada».)

Una vegada
passà un miseriós al meu enfront –
barba i cabells guarnits de polseguera
i un trèmul dit amenaçant el món.
Veia i cridava, però ell no hi era,
ni en els seus ulls ni en l'abrandada veu.
El voltaven minyons fent-ne riota.
«La branca el tusta; per fangueres trota».
«Odre de vi, ¿de quin celler torneu?»
I d'una pedra el va ferir la punta
i ell no es temia de son cap sagnant:

The senile potter no longer uses new moulds;
the early-rising old woman does her chores routinely.
Steel me against Your shuddering
like one who, on starting to eat bread,
has no other thought than breaking his bread,
like one so unfeeling that he no longer yearns,
like one who does not ever grieve
for what will never happen.

'Time was, Jehovah, when my night was not oppressed,
neither was I drawn abruptly to every unexpected path.
I had my job; towards my known skills
I was quietly pushed each day by the morning breeze.
I lived in my village, close to the woods;
and craved for the comforting thought
of buying the vineyard on the hill-side.
Having established myself I would search for a wife
and, under shelter of night, I would sow progeny.
(It is good for a man to have a home
so that on returning from his labours,
he can sit on the threshold star-gazing,
while his wife gently draws near and says
huskily: "I'm grateful to have been born".)

'One day
a destitute man crossed my path,
beard and hair decked with dust,
and with a trembling finger threatening the world;
seeing and shouting, yet not existing,
neither in his eyes nor in his ardent voice.
Mocking youths surrounded him:
"The branch hits him; he rushes about in the mud."
"Wineskin, from what cellar do you come?"
A sharp stone hit him on the head,
and he disregarded the bleeding:

pel viu de llum que cel i terra ajunta
anava ple de Déu tomballejant.

I jo tornant a agafar l'eina
vaig regraciar-te, Iahvè,
pel llogarret quiet i per la feina
i el ràfec de ma fe,
i la llei teva d'incessant cantúria
i els manaments, ombreig de mon camí –
perquè no mai em malmenés la fúria
com la busca en el cor d'un remolí.

Llavors per tres anyades malsegures
desferen l'hort la pedra i les malures
i el blat se'm va neulir;
em robà les ovelles de la pleta
un príncep que la tenda tragina per l'areny;
i jo, ferit d'una sageta,
farfallava com un que no té seny.

¿Què em valgueren treballs i paciències
i haver el voler de Déu salmodiat
i haver sotjat la llei i haver servat
la complicació de les obediències?
Ai de qui, just, s'alzina com déu de pedra, august!
Quan Déu revé, quan Déu es lleva
despulla l'home de la seva
pretesa d'ésser just.
Fui arrencat al bàndol
de l'honorada gent.
«Sigues rebuig», digué la Veu, «sigues escàndol
per a virtuts corcades en l'acontentament.
Dels bandejats la vida t'és prou bona;
per viaranys sense roderes aniràs;
a qui t'haurà parlat dirà la seva dona:

along the ribbon of light that bridges heaven
and earth, staggering he went on, full of God.

'And I, gathering my tools,
thanked Thee, Lord,
for my quiet village, for my work,
for the shelter of my faith,
for the unceasing drone of Your law,
and for the shadow of Your commandments as I went;
so that fury should never ill-treat me
as if I were a dust-speck within the heart of a whirlwind.

'But then came the uncertain years:
hail and disease blighted the orchard,
and the corn wilted;
a prince who pitches his tent here and there
thieved my sheep in their pen;
while I, wounded by an arrow,
was mumbling like a madman.

'What have I gained for my pains and patience,
and to have sung in praise of God's will,
and to have kept to the law and to have observed
the complexities of obedience?
Heaven help those who, in justice, stand straight like
      a stone god, majestic!
When God reappears, when God raises Himself,
He divests man of his
pretence of being just.
I was wrested from the company
of honourable people.
"Be a cast-off", the Voice said, "be an affront
to virtues rotten in their smugness.
Your life of exile is not that bad;
through unmarked paths you will go;
to the man that spoke to you his wife will say:

"¿Amb aquest home et fas?"
I tu, mal que et defengui llur sostre gent avara
i bordin gossos i xacals a ton trepig,
dóna mal d'ull a la bellesa clara
i infecta de misèria la joia i el desig,
car ja tota mirada, o radiant o llosca,
s'acalarà de sobte, bleïda per la fe:
vindré com terratrèmol o com gropada fosca
perquè Jo sóc, Jo sol, Iahvè!»

I així he anat pel món, pollós, amb tos preceptes,
embarbollant-me en figuracions,
dient els teus desdonaments i reptes
a reis i nacions.
Bon goig de jeure entre la palla poca
i del pa encetat i sobrer
i de la mel de la balmada soca
i de les móres d'esbarzer.
Però las, ensonyat, o bleixant per drecera,
en basarda de nit o en albades de plors,
només pensava a fer ton grat, quan era
més valent el meu cos.
«Iahvè m'ha abassegat», diguí; «sa força lleva
més pura encara en un escarbotat anap.
La pobresa atueix cada hora meva,
però em redreça el cap.
El meu esguard de sol al món, que no s'acala,
ha vist les voliors de tota llei d'ocells;
i el meu parrac és el record d'una ala
i al vent que passa es mou com ells.
Millor, que els meus esquinços, les meves cantarelles,
m'allunyin de la porta dels amics;
i en rompiment amb les honors més belles,
jo ofengui el capcineig de les donzelles
i l'asseguda majestat dels rics».

'Are you on speaking terms with that kind of man?'
And you, in spite of miserly people denying you shelter
and dogs and jackals barking at your footsteps,
you are hostile to clear beauty
and poison joy and desire with misery,
since every look, be it radiant or dim,
will suddenly fade, scorched by faith:
I'll come as an earthquake or as a dark cloud
because I am, I alone, Jehovah!"

'Thus I've been wandering, lice-infested, with Your
     precepts,
chattering in parables,
uttering Your retractions and challenges
to kings and nations.
I'm happy enough to lie on a bed of straw
and to eat crumbs of bread
and honey from the hollowed tree-trunk
and berries from brambles.
But weary, drowsy, or panting along short-cuts,
fearing night or the weeping dawn,
my overriding thought has been to keep to Your laws,
when my body was braver.
"Jehovah has possessed me," I said; "His strength
rises even purer in a cracked cup.
Poverty blights all my hours
but it straightens my head.
My worldly solitary eyes, never humbled,
have seen the flight of myriad birds,
and my cloak is a wing remembered
that flutters in the air like a bird's wing.
Better that my rags and singsongs
should keep me away from my friends' door;
and that, disdaining flattering honours,
I should offend nodding young maids
or the assured majesty of the rich."

Iahvè, jo et vaig donar mes forces i mon lluc.
Ara, però, del que has manat mon cor deslliura.
Saps que voldria reeixir i no puc.
Tot sovint, no em donaren aixopluc
sinó l'arlot, les dones de mal viure;
i tot sovint era afrontat, jo malastruc,
per la gentalla que volia riure.
¿Què em valia de fer mil hores de camí?
El cap girava el docte vers son escrit més fi.
Els ximples t'escarnien amb llurs amistançades
al so de lira i flauta, llaüt i tamborí.
Passaves Tu darrera finestres entelades,
fluix, amb desesma de colpir.

¿I crides justament Jonàs? Só una deixia
del temps, tot coquinesa: mon cor secret volia
el dolç esplai que Tu li vas negar.
No res de noble en la viltat traspua,
com no hi ha força en la cua
d'un ca.
I encar, ¿per què et refies Tu, Déu, d'un trist que passa?
Bé ho sé: té un mal decantament la nostra raça;
ningú no et fa cabal,
i al pas de les centúries ta parla s'escarrassa
com si no fossis vàlid i només eternal.
Els homes cerquen d'altres déus en folles faules.
¿Per què no pegues falconada a llur destí?
Tu pots el mal, d'una mirada, consumir,
i t'entretens en les bones paraules.
Digues-me, tot i que só tan mesquí,
¿com és que permeteres
que sigui corcuitós el mal, el bé tardà?
Al tros et roben les garberes
i Tu hi entres a l'hora foscant, a espigolar.

'Jehovah, I gave You my strength and my wits.
Now, however, my heart is free from Your commands.
You well know that I want to succeed yet I cannot.
Often the only shelter I received was
from bawds and prostitutes;
and often I was set upon, worse luck,
by a villainous crowd making fun of me.
Was it worth those thousand journeying hours?
The scholar devotes his attention to his writing.
Idiots with their mistresses would mock You
to the sound of lyre and flute, tambourine and lute.
You walked past misty windows,
weak, hesitating to knock.

'Are You just in summoning Jonah? I'm a wreck
of time, thoroughly mean; my secret heart wished for
the sweet warmth that You withheld.
Nothing noble arises from villainy,
nor is there strength in the tail
of a dog.
Furthermore, why did You, Lord, rely on this miserable
    traveller?
I know it well: our race has taken a wrong turn;
nobody heeds You,
and as the centuries pass Your voice is strained,
as though You were only eternal, not real.
Men are in search of other gods and foolish legends.
Why do You not seize their destiny?
With one glance You can scorch evil,
and yet You waste time with good words.
Tell me, granted that I am so mean,
how is it that You have allowed
evil to scamper and goodness to amble?
'The corn is stolen from Your field
and You go there in the evening to glean.

Tu que comandes legions sens nombre
te'n vas en seguiment del traïdor,
com si fossis no pas el seu Senyor
sinó la seva ombra.
Ningú veure't no cuida
de la gernació que encara et sent,
i fas com la finestra al baterell del vent
en una casa buida.
Ni ta amenaça esglaia ni ton consol revifa,
i menys ardit se't veu,
com l'home que vol vendre una catifa
i que en rebaixa el preu . . . –

   (Oh Nínive, ciutat potent i vilipesa,
ciutat guarnida amb mil carcasses de ciutats,
perpal de Déu quan li traïm la fe promesa! –
Per tos carrers adelerats
¿qui sentiria el meu parlar sinó els albats?)

   (Però bé cal que plegui ara
vara i sarró:
qui té el sarró i la vara
es pot passar de companyó.
El vent xiulà per la cinglera
i ara amb prou feines mou un brot:
quan hom té espera
s'encalma tot.
Sembla partida
aquella Veu que el manament em féu.
Potser m'oblida
Déu.
No he sentit pas la Veu de pura pensa;
i pot tornar a venir.
Vara, sarró, vingueu amb mi:
em faria temença
de restar ací.

You, who command numberless legions,
follow the traitor
as if You were not his Lord,
but his shadow.
Of the multitude that still hears You
no one bothers to seek Your presence,
and You act like a window battered by the wind
in an empty house.
Neither Your threats frighten nor Your comfort revives,
and You appear less resolute,
like one that wanting to sell a rug
brings down the price . . .

'(O Nineveh, accursed and powerful city,
embellished with the skeletons of a thousand cities,
God's big stick when we betray the promised faith!
Going along your bustling streets
who but children would listen to my voice?)

'(It is time now for me to pick up
staff and sack:
whoe'er has sack and staff
can do without companion.
The wind had been howling in the craggy rocks
and now a bough barely moves:
when one has learned to wait
all becomes calm.
The Voice that commanded me
appears now cut off.
Perhaps God
has forgotten me.
I've not heard the Voice of pure thought;
yet it can still recur.
Staff, sack, let's go:
to remain here
is to fear again.

A l'ase fer serviran les despulles
del jaç que deixo . . . ¿Sóc alliberat,
o bé la Veu roman entre les fulles
a punt de repetir la seva voluntat?
Semblen quietes les muntanyes.
Tot en son lloc, ni un branquilló malmès.
I total sento un murmuri de canyes . . .
un borinot . . . no res.)

The wild ass will find use for the scraps
of my bed of straw . . . Am I free,
or is it that the Voice is hiding among the leaves
ready to pronounce His will?
The mountains seem peaceful.
Everything is in its place, not a twig is broken.
All I hear is a murmur of reeds . . .
a bumble-bee . . . nothing.)'

II

Home perdut entre un manyoc de vies,
oh malaventurat!
A mig camí no tens esment de què volies.
Car travessem la fosquedat
dels nostres dies
com la sageta, dreta vers el destí ignorat.

Jo, boca ressonant tramesa a vèncer
pobles i reis, ara em voldria fonedís,
perdut, sense desig ni coneixença,
al fons d'una illa que un gran núvol protegís.
Qui em destriés, en l'hora
del meu antic renom,
de mi, baixet, parlava a qui tingués devora.
Ara no es torben en passant: só com tothom.
Poc em dol. Consirós de ma fugida,
del vianant m'allunyo sense greu,
car de la humanitat mon cor es desconvida:
terrible séc de Déu.
I en els plecs alterosos de la serra
m'embolcallen fonoll i tamarell;
que jo sigui secret com sota terra
és per desfici de l'imperi d'Ell.
I si jo poc sabés com Ell destria
al si mateix de l'ombra l'escàpol que el defuig,
en un clivell de roca em ficaria
o en el balmat d'un puig.

L'ànima meva en solitud desborda.
Oh erm! Dins mi s'animen converses quan m'atreus.
Més que el brogit la quietud eixorda:
tot cor és ple de veus.

II

'A man lost in a maze of paths,
O unfortunate man!
Midway you have lost all sense of purpose.
For we are traversing the obscurity
of our days
like an arrow, straight towards an unknown destiny.

'I, resounding voice aimed at conquering
peoples and kings, now I wish to vanish,
to be lost, free of desire or knowledge,
into the depths of an island covered by a big cloud.
Whoever caught sight of me,
when I was well known,
would whisper into the ear of his companion.
Now nobody stirs at my passing: I'm part of the crowd.
It hardly hurts. Conscious of my flight,
I do not mind avoiding the passer-by,
for my heart has forsaken being human:
God's terrible imprint.
And in the high recesses of the mountain range
fennel and tamarisk envelop me;
that I keep to myself as if buried
is out of unease with His authority.
As if I did not know that He can discern
the innermost shadow of anyone avoiding Him,
I'd hide in the fissure of a rock
or in the hollow of a mountain.

'In solitude, my soul overflows.
O wilderness! Dialogues with You revive within me.
More than noise stillness deafens me:
every heart is full of voices.

Jonàs no porta noves de Déu. La calma blava
de l'aire, a mes orelles consent d'endevinar
el vol de l'àngel que amorós em sol parlar:
em manca, però, l'àngel que mut m'acompanyava
amb un plec segellat a dins la mà.
I en l'endemig és cert que munta
a Nínive el pecat. El sol mateix
demana quan traspunta:
— ¿Cal veure encar la iniquitat que creix? —
I la nit bella i l'estelada clara
diuen, en llur estesa de repòs:
— ¿Hem de cobrir de pietat encara
un son sense perill i sense plors? —
Dins de la gran ciutat, no mai condreta,
la malvestat del riu cruel nega la gent.
D'un roc, Senyor, podries fer un profeta,
però ¿seràs darrera d'ell prou amatent?
Ton nom, Iahvè, perdura
i vius voltat de resplendor sens fi.
T'embadaleix de tos designis l'obra pura
i et reca de mirar com s'envilí.
I la druda del món encara folga;
un bruelar de víctimes fa trontollar l'espai,
i el dia es colga
en un abís d'esglai.
El crim és adorat en pedra i fusta.
Tes legions ¿on són?
De ton voler la vida es desajusta;
corren balders els falliments del món.
Passen cent anys i en ta bonança perseveres,
fins que ja el prec no flamareja, consumit;
però, puix Tu em creares i em mogueres,
també has volgut el meu neguit.
Es planyen fins les insensibles coses.

Jonah is no longer God's news carrier.
The blue calm of the air conjures up
wings of my talkative, loving angel:
I miss, though, the silent angel who once
    accompanied me
carrying a sealed fold of paper in his hand.
And all the while the certainty
of Nineveh's increasing sins. The sun itself
breaking over the horizon asks:
"Do we have to see again iniquity growing?"
And the beautiful night and the starlit sky,
in their immense repose, say:
"Do we have to smother with compassion again
a dream devoid of peril or tears?"
In the great city, corrupt as always,
the wickedness of the cruel river drowns its citizens.
Lord, from a rock You could create a prophet,
but would You be solicitous enough behind him?
Your name, Jehovah, is eternal
and You exist for ever surrounded by radiance.
Of all Your designs, purity of work gladdens You:
to see it debased grieves You.
The world's whore persists in her life;
a howling of victims shakes the air,
as the day sinks
into an abyss of terror.
Iniquity is worshipped in wood and stone.
Your legions, where are they?
Knowingly You bring life into disorder;
the world's errors run unchecked.
A hundred years have passed, and You persevere
    unperturbed
until prayer, consumed, no longer flickers;
but, since You created me and set me in motion,
You also willed my anxiety.
Even insensitive things feel sorrow.

¿Castigaràs tan sols qui implora ton redreç
i que el món sigui com Tu vols i Tu no imposes,
perquè a cada pecat t'enceles més?
L'aire suau debades faixa
amb l'arc de les promeses ton cor perdonador:
l'home té encara la mirada baixa:
por tinc, Senyor, que ja no et tinguin por.
¿Què hi fa, Iahvè, si mon pecat t'inspira
d'abatre sobre el món el teu enuig
i trenca la dormida de ta ira
un homenic que fuig?
Passada ja la treva,
que núvols de temperi coronin ton posat!
¿Què val la vida meva,
mal que ton peu l'esclafi, si tot és esclafat?

Un dia encalça l'altre dia:
la teva Veu no m'ha assolit enlloc.
La llum, distretament, no em coneixia,
ni res del món no m'ha parlat tampoc.
Temps era temps sabia
als matins si Tu m'eres avinent;
i la fullada, a l'hora foscant tota lleugera,
em deia: – Déu està content –;
i en el meu jaç, del colze meu darrera,
ton reny, en el corcó de mitjanit,
m'acompanyava, tot nuant-me el pit.
Cada fulla es movia a ta alenada,
cada silenci era un lloc religiós,
en cada flor sentia que hi era ta mirada
d'abans que el temps no fos.
I ja m'amaga, més que el bosc i la bardissa,
que et surti el compte sense l'inútil que se'n va.
Só cosa de tes mans llenegadissa,
pedra tornada al pedregar.

Will You punish only those who seek Your redress
and wish the world to be as You desire but do not ordain,
because with each sin You rise higher in heaven?
The mild air vainly tries to link
the archway of promises with Your forgiving heart:
man's eyes are still fixed downwards:
I fear, Lord, that You are no longer feared.
What does it matter, Jehovah, if my sins prompt You
to unleash over the world Your anger
and a little fugitive man thus breaks
Your passive wrath?
The truce now over,
let storm clouds crown Your countenance!
What is my life worth,
when Your foot crushes it, if all else is crushed?

'A day pursues another day:
Your voice nowhere reaches me.
The light, absentmindedly, did not recognize me,
neither has the world spoken to me.
Long ago I would know
in the morning if You were affable;
and leaves, slackening at twilight,
would say to me: "God is pleased";
and in the middle of the night, stretched in bed,
hands behind my head, Your reprimand
persisted in suffocating me.
Every leaf stirred at Your breath,
each silence was a worshipping moment,
in each flower I divined Your glance
from before the beginning of time.
And now, more than by thickets or woodlands,
I'm concealed by Your wish to dispense with me,
        a worthless fugitive.
I'm in Your hands a slippery thing,
a stone that's returned to the quarry.

Em cal seguir l'anguniat viatge
fins que no m'heguis més.
Fugir de Tu migra el coratge
pitjor que dar-se a dona o cavil·lar diners:
perxò l'ànima es plau d'ésser mesquina,
car Tu vols l'ardent i l'ardit;
i així per a tos ulls seré una mota fina:
que quan jo més m'amago de Tu més só petit.

I quan imperceptible no et donaré més pena,
potser diràs:
— Qui sap si fou Jonàs —,
tot contemplant l'abisme que empares amb ton braç
i on passa temorenc tot ço que viu i alena.
I ja hauràs esborrat, oh Déu, el teu rescripte
quan a Jaffa, d'on surt
el munt flairós de cedres cap al gran riu d'Egipte,
dins una nau distreta jo passi sense aürt,
i cabdellant-me dins l'estiba em faci curt.
I amb mon enyor per únic adjutori
(a la desesma teva: la sort, obedient),
d'allí viatjaré fins que m'exori
davant la proa, assolellat, un promontori
amb petges d'una raça diferent.
O potser tot serà caiguda i agonia
i finaré de la tempesta en el renou;
o em reprendràs com fa l'amant amb qui el traïa,
amb goig i amb ira que en els braços clou.
D'ençà que Adam del fruit de l'arbre tingué enveja
que ens trasbalsem i ens penedim.
Déu, que fa l'arbre, el destraleja:
i els nostres pensaments no són sinó corquim.

I have to keep up with my agonizing journey
until I'm out of Your reach.
To escape from You undermines my courage
worse than whoring or pondering over money:
this is why one's soul takes pleasure in being mean,
for You favour those who are fiery and bold;
thus to Your eyes I shall be an invisible speck,
since the more I hide from You the smaller I become.

And when made imperceptible I'll cease to pain You,
You will probably say:
"Did Jonah ever exist?"
while You contemplate the abyss shielded by Your arm
and where every living creature passes in fear.
And You'll have erased, O God!, Your decree
when at Jaffa, from where the scent of cedars
wafts towards Egypt's great river,
inside an unnoticed vessel I sail quietly
crouching in the hold, shrinking.
And with longing as my only baggage
(and with Your unconcern, following my luck),
I'll travel forward to the prow, in the sun, until
freed by a headland
trodden by another race.
Or perhaps agony and ruin will prevail,
and I shall die in the clamour of the tempest;
or You'll reprimand me as a betrayed lover would,
with joy and anger that an embrace will seal.
From the time that Adam envied the fruit on the tree
we have worried and regretted.
God, who made the tree, chops it down:
and our thoughts are no more than sawdust.'

III

¿Què em va llevar d'haver fugit,
d'amagar-me amb el braç, de pensar si no hi eres,
i en el fons de la nau d'estibar-me arraulit?
Tu ens rebateres
des de l'eixut un vent enfureït.
Tota la mar era un bull de venjança
i un frenesí de veus.
Quèiem al fons d'un clot llisquent, sense esperança;
muntaven serralades, d'un sol aüc, dempeus,
i eixordaven el cel en estimbant-se.
Asclada d'una arpada sa virtut,
dins una onada l'arbre major negà son greuge.
Al crit d'«Alleuja, alleuja!»,
va per la borda a peces tot l'aparell batut.
I en tal destret de malvolent fortuna,
l'un mariner sagnava del front, l'altre del queix;
i com si ja els arrossegués la fossa bruna
cridava cadascú son déu: el Sol, la Lluna,
el gran Bicorne, l'Hòrrea, un penyalot o un peix.
Un mal trontoll em va ferir la testa:
i el tenebrós folcat de la tempesta,
de la mort meva encobeït,
flairava la incertesa del fil de mon sentit.
I va durar el meu son en la terrabastada
fins que el patró va dir-me, de bursada:
— Alça't, crida el teu déu d'una vegada;
fibla son pensament, fes-lo girar;
ell és potser qui posa la cella corrugada:
i quan et vegi ens salvarà —.

III

'What did I gain by escaping,
by hiding under my arm, by imagining You did not exist,
by crouching in the hold of the ship?
You sent out
against us a great wind from the dry land.
The sea was a raging fury of vengeance
and a frenzy of voices.
We sank to the bottom of a slippery pit, without hope;
a mountainous sea swelled upwards, crested,
and tumbled down in a deafening crash.
Splintered by the slap of a wave,
the main mast toppled over.
At the shout: "Ease, ease!"
block and tackle went overboard.
And in such extreme distress of ill-fortune,
one sailor bled from his forehead, another from the jaw;
and as though already sinking into the dark grave,
each one of them was invoking his own god: the Sun,
        the Moon,
the great Bicorn, Ortygia, a boulder or a fish.
A dreadful jolt wounded my head:
in the sombre stampede of the storm,
I was in despair of my own life,
and I felt the thread of my senses breaking.
And in the turmoil I lay unconscious
until the skipper abruptly shouted:
"Get up, invoke your God once and for all;
sting His thoughts, change His mind;
perhaps He is frowning upon us,
and once He sees you we shall be saved."

Vaig pujar al pont, cama-segat d'angúnia,
i deia un remitger darrera meu:
— El cel es fa nit negra de rancúnia.
Algú d'aquesta nau ha enfuriat son déu.
Perdem el fust, el guany sonant, la vida clara;
torreja cada onada més amunt;
els monstres de la mar udolen en gatzara.
¿Finarem tots per culpa d'un?
Ens cal saber per què la nau trontolla
a rampeu de la mort.
Veniu, pareu la cridadissa folla:
en ròdol aplegats tirem la sort —.

I jo vaig ésser
tot d'una descobert com l'enemic cercat:
la sort revessa
m'havia assenyalat.
I duien pressa,
tots blancs de la quimera i amb espignets de por;
desfeien i refeien la conspiració
en un entra-i-surt de frisança.
— Ara sabrem què fas en la nau, traïdor,
les teves arts i la teva astrugança:
digues la teva llei, la teva nació.

— Jo poruc, jo l'amagat a l'estiba
(car de la llum i tot vivia en trist recel),
us obriré el meu cor davant la mort que arriba.
Sóc de la terra i la fe d'Israel,
nat al rocall i la garriga calcinada;
i adoro Iahvè, Déu del cel,
solitari Senyor de l'estelada
que va fer la mar i l'eixut;
i só per Ell menat i fora d'Ell perdut.

'Anxiously I went up to the bridge, knees shaking,
and behind me a crew member ranted:
"The sky is becoming a black night of rancour.
Someone in this ship has enraged his god.
We are losing the ship, our livelihood, the clear life;
each wave towers more than the last;
sea-monsters howl horrifically.
Shall we all die because of one man?
We must know why the ship is tossing
and about to founder.
Come, all of you, stop the mad shouting:
let's get together and cast lots."

'And all of a sudden I was
exposed as the enemy within:
ill luck
had pointed at me.
And they were all in a hurry,
white with anguish and rasping fear:
they came, following their conspiracy,
with hesitant urgency:
"Now we shall know what you are doing in the vessel,
     traitor,
your arts and your ill luck:
tell us, what is your law, your nation."

' "I, the frightened one hiding in the hold
(for even of the light I lived in fear),
as I face death I'll bare my heart to you.
I belong to the land of Israel and its faith,
born in the rubble of calcinated scrub-land;
I worship Jehovah, the God of Heaven,
solitary Lord of celestial bodies,
who made the sea and the dry land;
by Him I am guided, without Him I'm nothing."

– En pujant a la nau, ¿quin mal ordies?
– He pujat a la nau per fugir de Iahvè.
Cercava tortes vies,
esquiu al compliment de son voler.
Bé hauria repetit son nom en les pregàries,
però lluny, en la pau, com qui pren encantàries,
sense sofrir
ni penedir,
sense ésser desvetllat amb un ensurt i témer
ni de l'anunci confiat haver de trémer
ni arreplegar l'afront a cada trist camí
ni córrer món debades,
i mai per mai en núvols ni fulles ni flamades
sentir la Veu que m'escollí –.

I respongueren gent de la marineria:
– Quan és un Déu tan fer com Iahvè s'ha mostrat,
si li ve un pensament de gelosia
foll és qui no li lliuri el seu caragirat.
La voluntat, però, de ton Déu ens eixorda
i no sabem què mana amb tant de vent entorn.
– Aferreu-me – vaig dir, – tireu-me per la borda,
i veureu la bonança fent retorn.
Perquè en dol acabà ma fugida
i sóc en ma viltat avergonyit
i sé que Déu em crida
i que la mar es reinflà a son crit –.
De por, però, de pietat llur veu trencada,
van dir: – Potser son Déu se li voldrà amainar –.
Tot home prengué el rem a la desesperada
cap a la costa, en núvols i escuma embolcallada:
la mar encara amb més delit muntanyejà.

"When you came aboard, what evil were you plotting?"
"I thought the ship would hide me from Jehovah.
Reluctant to obey His wishes,
I was trying to find ways to escape.
I would certainly have repeatedly sung His name in
        my prayers
but from a distance, in peace, like someone chanting
        an incantation,
neither suffering
nor repenting,
free of sudden awakenings and without fear
of the entrusted announcement,
nor did I have to gather insults on every wretched path,
nor undertake journeys in vain,
and never, never in clouds, leaves or leaping flames
hear the Voice that had chosen me."

'And the sailors replied:
"When such a brave God as Jehovah has revealed
        Himself,
if jealousy crosses His mind,
it would be foolish for anyone not to surrender a traitor.
The will of your God, though, deafens us,
and in this howling wind we don't know what He wants."
"Seize me" I said, "throw me overboard,
and you'll find calm seas returning.
Because my running away ended in distress,
and I am ashamed of my villainy
and I know that God is calling me
and that the seas swell upwards at His behest."
In fear, though, with piety and broken voice,
they said: "Perhaps his God will listen to him."
Desperately all hands took up oars towards
the coast covered in mist and spray;
the sea briskly became mountainous.

Els rems caigueren de les mans. Llavores
feren els homes a Iahvè llur gran clamor:
— Tu que ens castigues i ens acores
i ens deixes capolats, sense braó,
Déu de cella feresta!,
Tu que, en havent badat la fossa que va i ve,
ens rebolques al bat de la tempesta
pel trist encauament d'un fugisser:
si fina l'home que volies
no ens neguis en l'abís!
És cosa teva si has pensat que et venjaries.
Ets Tu qui diu: «Així».
No el llencem a la mar, ets Tu qui el llences;
si pares l'altra mà, ben cert que l'heus.
Pots fer-li una altra nau si t'hi repenses,
o posar-li una illa sota els peus —.

I, guany diví de la llarga palestra,
fui tirat a la mar. En aldarull:
— Vejam — deien les veus — si Déu el cull —.
I ja el cel amarat eixí en finestra,
perdé la mar son bull.

En la planura abonançada
un gran peix que Iahvè prop de mi féu saltar,
d'una bocada,
mig cloent els ulls, m'envià.
Jo, quan la nau vela a Jaffa prenia
— els folls cantaven, reien els ardits —,
amagatall per al meu cor volia;
però Déu trabucà ma traidoria
i aní a l'amagatall per als sentits:
i en el ventre del peix romania,
alliberada l'ànima, tres dies i tres nits.

Oars dropped from their hands. Then
the men voiced forcefully their appeal to Jehovah:
"You who are punishing and tormenting us
and leave us exhausted, spiritless,
God of fierce brow!,
having opened up the unsteady rocking grave, You
have thrown us helpless to the mercy of the storm
because a miserable fugitive is hiding from You:
if the man who is hiding dies,
do not drown us in the abyss!
It is Your concern if You seek revenge.
It is You who says: 'Thus',
It is not us who cast him into the sea; it is You.
If You reach out the other hand, surely You can save him.
You could build him another ship if You wished,
or You could lay out an island under his feet."

'And, divine gain of the long contest,
I was thrown into the sea. In disorder:
"Let's see" the voices said "if God picks him up."
And as the drenched sky stretched out clear,
the sea abated.

'In the levelled sea
a great fish, which Jehovah sprung up before me,
casually,
swallowed me up.
When I set sail from Jaffa —
the foolish were singing, the bold were laughing —
I was seeking a shelter for my heart;
but God overturned my treachery
sending me to a hideout for my person;
and in the belly of the fish I remained,
my soul at peace, for three days and three nights.'

IV

Ni el pèlag que s'abissa ni el vent ja no em fan nosa.
Mon seny en la fosca reneix.
Ja só dins una gola més negra, millor closa;
    i crec, dins el ventre d'un peix.

S'han esvaït, d'una bocada a l'embranzida,
    ma petitesa, mon esglai.
Re no em distreu, dubte no m'heu, desig no em crida:
    Déu és el meu únic espai.

Vaig, d'una empenta, sota la rel de les muntanyes
    o só llençat, d'un cop rabent,
a l'aigua soma: allí va dibuixant llivanyes
    l'estel en l'escata batent.

Déu juga. Déu ens tira lluny i mai no ens llença.
    Canto son nom amb veu igual,
orb, doblegat, com esperant una naixença
    dins la cavorca sepulcral.

Al manament de Déu neguí les meves passes.
    — Qui et fos — vaig dir-li — inconegut! —
Perxò sóc en les ones, car elles, jamai lasses,
    de fer i refer tenen virtut.

Ell en l'abís de tot sement mon cos embarca
    perquè hi reneixi per a Ell.
I jo hi só refiat com Noè en la seva Arca
    i Moïsès en el cistell.

IV

'Neither towering seas nor wind trouble me anymore.
    In the darkness my senses revive.
I'm within the blackest gorge, firmly enclosed;
    and, in the belly of a fish, I have faith.

'My meanness, my fear, have vanished
    in the impulse of a straight gulp.
Nothing distracts me, no doubts assail me, no desire
       calls me:
    God is my only abode.

'I'm pushed under the roots of mountains
    or thrown by a fierce blow
towards shallow waters: there the star draws
    fissures on the throbbing scales.

'God plays. God flings us far, but never away.
    With even voice I sing His name,
blind, doubled up, as if waiting for a new life
    within the sepulchral tomb.

'To God's command I denied my steps.
    "If only I were," I said, "unknown to You!"
That's why I'm in the waves, for they, never at rest,
    in their constant ebb and flow have virtue.

'In the abyss of all seed God embarks my body
    so that I may be reborn for Him.
And I feel as secure as Noah in his Ark,
    or Moses in the basket.

Oh lassos peus, oh mes cansades vagaries,
no m'haveu dat sinó dolors.
Sense l'angoixa ni la càrrega dels dies
com el no nat sóc a redós.

I si el meu seny es priva de signes il·lusoris,
dins l'impossible visc ardit.
I un dia, en llur follia, els savis hiperboris
diran que aquest peix no ha existit.

'O tired feet, O my wearisome wanderings,
　　I've had only pain from you.
Free from anguish or daily burdens,
　　I feel sheltered like an unborn child.

'If my senses reject illusory signs,
　　within the impossible I live resolute.
And one day, hyperborean learned men, in their folly,
　　will proclaim that this fish never existed.'

V

Bell era de veure
altre cop el batre exaltat,
la pressa
del petit en l'il·limitat,
l'ocell en els aires,
el peix en el ròdol marí,
la gran vastedat que com la del cel no podríeu
saber, mesurar ni tenir;
bell era de veure que el fàcil s'eixampla,
i enllà l'impossible se us fa transparent.
Ocell, tu que et daures del dia,
i peix que degotes l'argent,
un goig en el cor se us aboca
llampant i lluent.
Oh joia
del petit en l'il·limitat!
Enfora de greus agonies
jo em veia al gran aire llençat,
del clos de la fosca tornat
dins una llargada de dies.

Tot era al món començament i joventut.
La mar mirallejava només per a un llagut.
Jo veia l'or del dia que sobre el mar s'escola.
En una cala, prop d'un pi, la negra gola
m'havia tirat a l'eixut.
Sentia olor de sal i olor de ginestera;
lluïa al sol un home pel turó
i anava a jeure en el tendal d'una figuera;
un fuminyol pujava damunt d'un cabanó.
— Ací — vaig dir — jo restaria
com l'arbre, com el roc —. Però la Veu vingué:

V

'It was good to witness again
life's throbbing exuberance,
the haste
of the small in the limitless,
the bird in the air,
the fish in the open sea,
the great vastness which like that of the sky
one could not conceive, measure or possess;
it was good to witness how the easy expands,
and in the distance how the impossible becomes
    transparent.
Bird touched by the gold of day,
fish dripping silver,
a gladness of heart bursts out,
gloriously bright.
O joy
of the small in the limitless!
Free from deep anguish
I felt driven to the freedom of the air,
having returned from dense darkness
towards unending days.

'The world was new and full of promise.
The sea was reflecting a lone felucca.
I saw the golden day lengthening over the sea.
I had been thrown from inside the black gorge
onto dry land, in a small bay, where a pine tree stood.
I sensed the smell of salt and broom flowers;
lit up by the sun, a man walked along the hill
towards the shade of a fig tree;
smoke climbed from a shack.
"Here," I said, "I would rest,
like the tree, like the rock." But the Voice came:

– Vés a l'esclat de Nínive, Jonàs, no passis dia:
plegats, tu arribaràs i Jo diré –.

I em vaig alçar. Del roc l'ardència,
del pi l'aroma m'ignoraven el posat.
S'esvaïa tot tracte del lloc amb ma presència
com si ja hagués pres comiat.
Son gust d'embadalir perdia la mar blava;
mudà el jaient un núvol com si l'esquena em des;
sentia l'aire que es desficiava
i la mota de pols em deia: – Vés –.

I en aquell punt vaig ésser
com picat d'escurçó diví:
em va sobtar i em va garfir,
em va corprendre i consumir
la pressa.
En delerosa caminada,
sota l'assolellada
em retornava el brot de romaní;
i en fosquejant, quan em sentia deixondir,
em redreçava el cap l'amor de l'estelada
on era escrit el manament diví.
De mon trigament en revenja
feia com l'home que d'un sol neguit és ple:
dormir com qui no dorm, menjar com qui no menja,
fer via sense veure, sentir sense saber.
Era ma força i ma sola esperança
el mot que Déu m'havia dit.
I aquell mot repetia dia i nit
com un amant llaminejant amb delectança,
com un infant que va cantant per por d'oblit.
Cap arbre no em parava, cap casa no em prenia,
tot quant topava era darrera meu llençat,
i caminava nit i dia:
no veia més que pols roent o fosquedat.

"Jonah, do not pause, go unto glittering Nineveh:
together we shall go, you'll appear, I shall speak."

And I stood up. The heat of the rock,
the scent of the pine, ignored my stance.
The connection with my presence was broken,
as though I had already departed.
The blue sea lost its fascination;
a cloud moved sideways as if turning its back on me;
I felt the restless air,
and a cluster of dust said: "Go."

'And at that moment, I was
as if stung by divine venom:
it startled me and it seized me,
it enraptured me and spurred
my haste.
Walking along eagerly
under the burning sun
a rosemary sprig revived me;
and at the close of day, when I felt of good cheer,
lovingly towards the starlit sky I turned my head
to see there God's written command.
Atoning for my prevarication
I behaved like a man burdened with a single anxiety:
sleeping and not resting, eating without hunger,
walking without seeing, feeling and not knowing.
My strength, my only hope, was
the word given by God to me.
I kept saying that word day and night,
savouring it with relish as a lover would,
like a child chanting it for fear of forgetting.
No tree halted me, no house tempted me,
all that came my way was thrown behind me,
and I walked day and night:
all that I saw was burning dust and darkness.

Mon viatge en xardor, perill, dejuni
durà de pleniluni a pleniluni,
i l'esperó diví feia mes plantes lleus.
Amb res mos ulls no feren pacte
ni va tenir ma boca tracte:
soldat complint un manament exacte
no s'entrebanca de lligams ni adéus.

Però tantost la quarta lluna era passada,
malaltia cruel fou mon camí:
si deturava un punt la caminada
no em sabia tenir.
Vermelles del sol les parpelles,
mes passes eren cada cop menys amatents;
empolsegades la barba i les celles,
feixugues les espatlles i mos badius ardents.
Les coses avinents semblaven en llunyària,
s'esgarriava l'esma dins la cremor del cap;
mon peu sagnava; malgirbaven llur pregària
el tèrbol seny, la llengua eixuta com un drap.
I vaig sentir un matí que la claror del dia
dintre ma testa feia com l'abellot que brum,
i ma mirada al raig de sol s'agemolia,
malrecaptosa de la llum.
Volia, tot pensant: — Iahvè t'espera —,
refer-me en nou delit;
però topant en pedra travessera,
a terra vaig trobar-me, colgat en polseguera,
i no sabia com alçar-me, estamordit.
— ¿Fuig Nínive de mi? — vaig saber dir-me encara;
i per fer-me, batut, un poc de nit,
entre les mans vaig recerar la cara.

My journey, all heat, peril and fasting,
lasted from full-moon to full-moon,
and the divine spur made my feet lighter.
My eyes did not fix on anything,
I did not exchange words with anyone:
a soldier carrying out a definite command
does not encumber himself with friendships or goodbyes.

But soon after the moon's first quarter was passed,
my journey became a cruel affliction:
if I halted my step awhile
I could not stand upright.
My eyelids were red from the sun's glare,
my steps gradually became less eager;
my beard and eyebrows were decked with dust,
my shoulders heavy, my nostrils afire.
Nearby things seemed far away,
inside my burning head reason went astray;
my feet were bloodied; my brain was confused,
and with my tongue parched like a rag, I muddled
    my prayers.
One morning I felt the light of day
buzzing inside my head like a drone,
with my eyes lowered in the sun's rays,
fearful of the light.
By thinking "Jehovah is waiting"
I hoped to renew my strength;
but stumbling over a stone
I fell down, covered in dust,
and, shattered, I knew not how to stand up.
"Nineveh, leave me alone!" I managed to say;
and beaten, I sought darkness
by covering my face with both hands.

Darrera meu un vell descavalcà d'un ruc.
— Alça't! Qui cau, si no s'aixeca, algú l'enterra.
Un covenet de figues i una verra
porto a ciutat. ¿Mai no l'has vista? Malastruc,
puja a cavall de l'ase. Poc tires per feixuc!
D'ací s'albira el lloc per on el riu aferra
la gran ciutat que talla i ascla i serra,
i abat les fites en el món poruc.
Ací l'home de cor occeix, empala, aterra;
els himnes de triomf són obra de l'eunuc.
Totes les arts acalen el front davant la guerra,
car és l'espasa jove i l'esperit caduc.
I dels mercats emplenen seguidament el buc
amb saques precioses la gent de coll feixuc;
i vénen dones de tota la terra,
les més perfectes en pit i maluc.
Assur és immortal, i el món una desferra —.

Ma testa amb pena es redreçà.
D'una torta del riu dellà
blanquejaven casals per la vorada;
i jo, de tort, com bèstia ferida, amb la mirada
que ho veia tot rodar,
vaig alçar el braç amb virior desesperada
del darrer pòsit de mon cor arrabassada;
i malversant-hi un any de vida vaig clamar:
— Quaranta dies més i Nínive caurà —.

'Behind me an old man dismounted from an ass.
"Stand up! He who falls and does not rise will be buried.
I'm taking a basket of figs and a sow
to the city. Have you ever been there? Wretched man,
come and ride on the ass; you don't look too heavy!
From here you can see where the river clasps
the great city and cuts, splits, indents,
and in a fearful world demolishes boundaries.
Here the caring man kills, impales, knocks down;
the triumphant hymns are the work of the eunuch.
Facing war the Arts submit,
because the sword is young and the spirit old.
In the markets men of weighty head
fill their precious sacks;
and women of all nations, those with perfect
hips and breasts, flock into the city.
Asshur is immortal, and the world a wreck."

'With difficulty I lifted my head.
Beyond a bend in the river
whitened houses appeared;
and I, staggering like a wounded beast that sees
the world whirling round,
with desperate vigour wrenched from
the last dregs of my heart, I raised my arm;
and remembering a wasted year of my life, I cried out:
"Forty more days and Nineveh will fall."'

VI

Enmig de runes tristes
— jaç de l'esperitat o cau de l'assassí —
un rec, de la ciutat a les envistes,
em mostra, igual que un dit, el meu camí.
Ara veig que no anava a la perduda.
El sol tot just comença a davallar.
Cal que m'adreci al sol vivent que hi ha:
una rònega dona ajaguda
al peu de son llindar.

JONÀS

¿Qui ets, entremesclada
de vels i de cabells,
desistiment de tot, erta a l'entrada
del teu derroc, devora els joncs vermells?
Sense honrament els nostres caps groguegen
i encara só malalt de mon camí:
però callem plegats, si més t'estimes
de no dir-me quin dol et derruí.

DONA

Estrany vivent, que encara et gires
a mi! No diré pas:
«Conta'm què cerques o de què fugires»,
car pitjor que no deixes trobaràs.
Els déus i els homes coneguí debades;
sembrat no hi ha en mon tros ni renadiu.
I l'aigua i jo dormim plegades
i només l'aigua viu.

VI

'Amidst mournful ruins —
lair of the possessed or assassin's hideout —
a watercourse, in sight of the city,
like a pointing finger, shows me the way.
I'm on the right road after all.
The sun is just beginning to sink.
I must speak to the only living being here,
an old woman in rags crouching
at the step of her threshold.'

JONAH

Who are you, forlorn woman,
enmeshed in veils and hair,
lifeless at the entrance
of your ruin, close to red reeds?
It is no dishonour that both our faces are ashen,
and I'm ill from my travels:
but let's be silent if you prefer
not to tell me what afflicts you.

WOMAN

Living stranger, who kindly
speaks to me! I'll not say:
'Tell me what are you seeking, and from what did you
    escape?'
because you'll find worse than what you left behind.
In vain I've known gods and men;
in my plot nothing grows,
water and I sleep together,
and only the water is alive.

JONÀS

¿És saviesa
de viure com tu fas?
La terra passa afany, el cel trontolla.
Qui gosaria dir: «Ja no et mouràs!»
No pas jo que, en mon jaç de ginesteres
arrabassat a un son pregon,
corro per a servir la Veu i m'esgarrio,
corro per a fugir-ne i és enfront.

DONA

Tot és follia,
córrer i estar, vetllar i dormir;
tot és engany de vides condemnades:
donar-se i escometre i resistir.
Sacerdotessa havia estat de l'Alba
damunt turons daurats:
és erm el lloc que enfistonà la vinya
i tots els meus parents són coltellats.

JONÀS

Lleu és l'aurora, que igualment sospira
d'ombres minvant, del sol arborador:
mai no té temps de voluptat ni d'ira;
fuig de la fosca i de l'esclat té por.
El déu potent és el tothora ardit
que amb el llamp les tenebres enlluerna,
o dels núvols cridant la baluerna
fa del migdia nit.

JONAH

Is it wise
to live as you do?
The earth is in turmoil, heaven trembles.
Who would dare say: 'You will not move ever again!'
Not I, who in deep sleep was wrenched
from my bed of broom branches.
I run to serve the Voice and I go astray,
I run away to evade it and it confronts me.

WOMAN

All is madness,
to run and to stay, to be awake and to sleep;
all is a deceit of damned lives:
to surrender, to attack, and to resist.
I was a priestess of the Dawn
above golden hills;
the vineyard is now wasteland,
and all my relatives have been slain.

JONAH

Weak is the dawn, which frets about
waning shadows, out of sight of the sun;
it never has time for voluptuousness or anger;
it avoids darkness and the sun's rays hurt.
The powerful God, ever bold,
with a flash of lightning illumines darkness,
or with thundering clouds
turns midday into night.

DONA

¿Sou el captaire que en la festa enuja
i encara amb do – perquè de tot s'està –
de fer venir la pluja
o bé d'esquivar el núvol cel enllà?
¿O sou el foll que el càstig nou celebra
per a un país poblat de gent i verd
i parla d'un sol déu – i trem de febre,
ple del tuf miserable del desert?

JONÀS

Serveixo el Déu vivent: sa mà trabuca
el reialme, les naus, el cor mesquí;
un cop m'esglaia, però torna i truca
ben dolç, pagat d'una conversa amb mi.
D'Ell ve la pau i Ell és el meu desfici:
sóc en ses mans cosa a desfer i refer.
Sé que vol l'invisible sacrifici.
¿Què hi fa si passo d'aquest món? Déu ve.

DONA

Déu que vol castigar, mai no destria;
ell perd l'estol, arrasa la ciutat;
mentre que l'home en son camí es doldria
fins del gemec d'un ca oblidat.
¿Què cerca a sotragades
aquest déu cellaadust?
Car dues coses han caigut plegades:
el que era Bell i el que era Injust.

WOMAN

Are you the beggar who spoils the feast,
who still has the gift – because of his abstinence –
to bring rain,
to shift clouds in the sky?
Or are you the fool who predicts punishment
to a green country crowded with people,
and speaks of the one and only God – and feverishly
    shakes,
reeking of the miserable desert stench?

JONAH

I'm a servant of the living God: His hand
upsets nations, ships, the wretched heart;
at times He frightens me, but then He comes back
gently, keen to converse with me.
He is the bringer of peace, and also of my anguish:
in His hands I'm a thing to manipulate.
I know that He wants the invisible sacrifice.
What does it matter if I leave this world? God follows.

WOMAN

A god who wants to punish, never descries;
he loses his flock, razes the city;
while a man on his way would even feel for
the whimper of an abandoned dog.
What is this sullen-browed god
so hesitantly seeking?
For two things have fallen simultaneously:
what was Beautiful and what was Unjust.

JONÀS

¿Qui es sent davant sos ulls l'ànima pura?

DONA

Ningú del món és bo.
Té, fins i tot el que més poc s'alçura,
cobejança en el prec, culpa en el plor.
Negre esperit que a l'esperit se'ns colla
a cadascú fa dir:
«La meva fe degolla:
un déu, pitjor que jo, s'agita en mi».

JONÀS

Jo més em temo que mon Déu declara
un pobre enuig de bon passar.
Qui sap si encara ens baixarà a acotxar
dolç i més dolç a tall de mare.
Però d'Ell sé una cosa: que m'arbora,
que el món no fóra més si Ell em deixés. –
Tu, ¿què mai adoraves en l'aurora,
que tot seguit no és?

DONA

Servia l'alba amb la libació
de les rosades,
i amb flors no encara a bastament badades
i sense taca ni pugó.
Car l'alba inspira en fonedís auguri
l'avís de cada recomençament,
la sorpresa de cada pensament
i l'encís de l'amor abans no duri.

JONAH

Who in his eyes feels the purity of his soul?

WOMAN

Nobody in the world is good.
Even the meekest reveals
covetousness when praying, guilt when weeping.
Black spirit that grips the mind
forcing each one of us to say:
'My faith beheads:
a god, worse than myself, stirs within me.'

JONAH

I'm afraid, rather, that my God shows
a mild annoyance, easily passed over.
Who knows if He will even tenderly descend
to tuck us up in motherly fashion?
But I know one thing of Him: that He sets me on fire,
that the world would no longer exist if He left me.
You, have you never worshipped
the evanescent dawn?

WOMAN

I served Dawn with a libation
of dew,
and flowers with newly opened buds,
free of pests or blemish.
Because dawn inspires with brief anticipation
the onset of each new beginning,
the fascination of each thought,
and the marvel of love before it ends.

Oh delicada, decebuda fe!
Oh inútil cura de sos dits de rosa!
De tota bella cosa,
tant com llarg el desig, és curt l'alè.
I sort si, com l'aurora, la bellesa
traspunta i fina sobre el món esquiu,
mai abastada ni escomesa.
És ben pitjor si viu.
Marcida al bat de l'aire,
ella, l'alada, d'immortal costum,
acabarà com la captaire
que s'humilia o maleeix la llum.
Arran del tracte, la viltat comença.
Tu sola ets pura, tu que passes lleu,
oh gràcia fugint sens defallença,
gemec dels homes i sospir d'un déu.

JONÀS

L'aurora tem de viure i es preserva
del goig, que la prendria adelerat;
¿qui es fiarà de la rosada en l'herba,
nada en secret i morta d'amagat?
I el celatge amb color d'enamorada,
i, a contrasol, el degotís lluent,
nasqueren una matinada
d'aquella immensa força pacient
que fa una serralada
on cal un roc per a la font planyent.
El llamp, el tro, la majestat revelen
de Iahvè corrugat. La seva amor
envia missatgers que el món encelen
en esperança i en enyor.
I havent temut dels àngels les espases,
m'esllangueixo la posta en contemplant,

O delicate, deceived faith!
O unavailing solicitude of its rosy fingers!
Of every beautiful thing
the greater the desire, the lesser the spirit.
And lucky if, like dawn, beauty
rises and dies over a hostile world,
beyond reach, never challenged.
It is much worse if it survives.
Withered in the open air,
She, the winged, immortal one,
will end her life like the beggar woman
who humbles herself or curses light.
Soon after a friendship, villainy begins.
You alone are pure, Dawn, you of brief passage,
O unfaltering, fugitive grace,
mankind's grief and a god's sigh!

JONAH

Dawn dreads life and shields itself
from joy, which would increase its brilliance;
who would trust the grass dew,
born in secret, dead in hiding?
And the sky tinted a languishing colour,
and dripping water bright against the sun,
were born at the break of a day
from the immense enduring force
of the mountain range,
where a rock-face is needed for the plaintive fountain.
Lightning and thunder unmask Jehovah's
displeasure. His love
sends messengers who lift the world
with hope and longing.
And fearing the swords of angels,
I slip away watching the sunset

car Iahvè dura pel camí de brases
roentes que es desfan. –

I ella restà ajaguda i jo partia.
Com volta de topazi, encara el dia
semblava tot suspès, i ja amb delit
cada arbre s'entendria
d'un fresc anunci de la nit.
I per a ella, en el seu cor premuda,
com per a mi, que anava al gran estrall,
era el record de la conversa haguda
per a nous pensaments un debanall.

for Jehovah's presence endures on my way
through incandescent, melting coals.

'And she stayed there, crouching, as I was leaving.
Like a topaz vault the sky lingered
as if in suspension, and anticipating delight
each tree softened
at the fresh heralding of night.
And for the woman, her heart constrained,
as it was for me on my way to the great destruction,
the remembrance of the words exchanged
provided us with solace and fresh thoughts.'

VII

Oh gran ciutat de Nínive! Seguir-te és un flagell.
De cap a cap demanes tres jornades.
De tos carrers ¿qui mai faria descabdell?
Qui comptarà tes torres, tes cúpules sagrades,
tos escamots llampeguejants,
tos pous voltats de dones, els crits de tos marxants,
tos gossos vora el munt de deixalles perdudes,
els bells joiells que fan dringar les teves drudes,
el nombre de llenguatges llunyedans
de camellers i mariners i vianants,
tos lleons adormits al clos, i tes panteres
que giravolten en afany captiu,
i tes palmeres,
ventalls del riu!
Deixa que miri encar ta joia fugitiva,
oh dea-estel entre la pols dels mons,
oh diamant de flama viva
entre deserts i devastacions! —

I feta una jornada per dins ciutat, fou hora
que jo clamés: — Acala't, mercè de Déu implora:
ho dic a qui s'atura i a qui rient se'n va.
Bateu els pits, oh dones; guerrers, llenceu l'espasa.
Car Déu m'arbora insuportable com la brasa.
Quaranta dies més i Nínive caurà.
No em deu ni un tros de pa, perquè Iahvè desola
les vostres llars: la bròfega perdició ja vola,
i temorós dels sostres que afonarà l'estrall,
seré com la ratxada de vent, sense abrigall;
beuré, bocaterrós, en una sequiola,

VII

'O great city of Nineveh! To cross you is torture.
From side to side three days are required.
Who could ever unravel the confusion of your streets?
Who could count your towers, your sacred domes,
your flashing marching soldiers,
your wells surrounded by women, the street cries of
    merchants,
your dogs near piles of discarded rubbish,
the graceful clinking jewels of your concubines,
the number of foreign languages
from camel-drivers, mariners, and passers-by,
your lions sleeping behind bars, your panthers
turning round in their captive restlessness,
and your palm trees
fanning the river!
Let me see awhile your fugitive joy,
O star-goddess set in the dust of the universe!
O diamond of living flame
surrounded by deserts and devastations!

'And after a day's walking about the town, it was time
for me to proclaim: "Bow down, implore God's mercy;
I am saying this to those who stop and to those who
    walk away laughing.
Beat your breasts, O women! Warriors, throw away
    your swords.
For God inflames me, unbearable like glowing embers.
Forty days more, and Nineveh will fall.
Do not give me even a chunk of bread, because Jehovah
lays waste your homes: harsh ruin is in the air.
And fearing fallen ceilings from the destruction to come,
I'll be like a gust of wind, without shelter;
I'll drink, face down, from a ditch,

viuré de roseguies del porc i del cavall.
Car jo no só del vostre lloc i parentela
ni vinc a les folgances de noble viatger:
sóc un avís, com la llum groga que s'encela
quan sobre el camp curull la pedregada ve,
com gemega el gos i recela
abans que el terratrèmol esberli son terrer,
com vent que apaga la candela
i tira a terra el candeler –.

I els anants i vinents cregueren ma paraula
perquè Iahvè era en mi;
i oblidaren llur llit i llur taula
i els féu basarda de robar i d'occir.
I sentiren un jou en l'espatlla abatuda
i un serrament de cor de nació vençuda:
i al palau de llur rei em van seguir
amb una fressa d'alirets sens fi.
I avant, entre les dones de túnica esquinçada
i els grans barbats injuriant-se els rulls,
llegia del palau damunt la portalada:
– Tem el llindar de la reial estada.
Deixa, en sortint, la llengua si no des d'ara els ulls –.

I en contemplant la nostra corrua adolorida
digué el cap de la guàrdia del rei:
– Feu pas, soldats. Ja sé que per antiga llei
no passarà la porta sens pena de la vida
home ni dona ni animal, llevat
qui a so de flauta, amb ornaments d'esclat,
fes al rei presentalla
de les despulles més brillants de la batalla
o bé lliurés son or o sa virginitat.
Però qui ve miseriós d'un llarg viatge,
colrat pel sol, esparracat pels vents,

I'll live on scraps of pork and horse-meat.
For I do not belong here nor am I related to you
nor do I come for the pleasures of a noble traveller:
I'm a herald, like the yellow light in the sky
predicting the approaching hail over laden fields,
like the moaning dog that senses and fears an earthquake
before the ground breaks,
like a wind that blows out a candle
and knocks down the candlestick."

And passers-by believed my word
because Jehovah was in me;
and they neglected their bed and their table
and they feared to rob or kill.
And they felt a weight on their dejected shoulders
and a heartache like that of a defeated nation:
and they followed me towards their king's palace
with prolonged loud shrieks.
And, ahead of me, among tunic-torn women
and the bearded great attacking their curls,
I read above the monumental doors of the palace:
"Fear the threshold of the royal house.
On the way out leave your tongue, if not, your eyes
    on the way in."

'And seeing that distressed crowd,
the officer in charge of the royal guard said:
"Let them pass, soldiers. I know that an ancient law says
that no man, woman or animal shall cross
the threshold without loss of life, except
those who, dressed ostentatiously, to the sound of a flute,
come to offer the king
the finest booty taken in battle
or to surrender their gold or their virginity.
But whoever comes destitute from a long journey,
sun-burnt, his clothes torn by the wind,

sense més arma que l'esguard salvatge
ni més cabal que un barboteig de nous accents,
bé pot portar un missatge
no pas de l'or i el flam dels nostres déus ardents,
sinó de la meitat de món que s'angunia
i passa fam i fred, horror i malaltia,
i que potser té déus encara més potents —.

I el rei va dir quan del gran tron fórem devora:
— ¿Qui deixa entrar el jueu
seguit d'una gentada que perd el seny i plora?
¿És que d'Istar la glòria sap greu
a qui dins casa de son fill s'acora?
D'un cop de bec
l'àguila puny l'ovella per sempre aquietada.
Més bella Istar que no la humanitat cansada,
avorreix el gemec.
Oh tu, fill del desfici
i l'ombra, com un rat-penat que vola en va,
¿qué et va contar Iahvè de dalt del precipici?

— Quaranta dies més i Nínive caurà.

— Istar al goig ens crida,
i a veure els averanys de gloriosa vida
a dins l'entranya sangonent de tot país,
oh fill de terra cor-entenebrida
on un Baal tot rústec intimida,
d'un muntitjol, el poble espantadís;
Istar al goig ens crida:
no pot desfer ta màgia son vesperal somrís.

— No compta pas l'imperi per al Senyor del cel
més que un romboll de polseguera,
i si la vera glòria del món covà Israel
ho féu en nit profunda i en migraments d'espera.

with no other weapon than his wild appearance,
and for sole baggage a burble of new accents,
can nevertheless be the bringer of a message,
not of gold and fire of our ardent gods,
but of half the anguished world,
a hungry and cold world, living in fear and sickness,
and with perhaps even more powerful gods."

'And as we approached the great throne, the king said:
"Who has allowed this Jew to come here
followed by a weeping, mindless crowd?
Is it that Ishtar's glory is regretted
by those who in their son's house find distress?
With one stroke of its beak
the eagle quietens the lamb for ever.
Fair Ishtar, more than tired humanity,
abhors moaning.
O you, born of anxiety
and darkness, like a bat that flies aimlessly,
what did Jehovah tell you from the precipice's height?"

'"Forty more days, and Nineveh will fall."

'"Ishtar urges us to rejoice,
and to behold signs of glorious life
within the bleeding heart of all countries,
O son of a dark-hearted land
where a rustic Baal intimidates,
from a hill-side, the timorous nation;
Ishtar urges us to rejoice:
your magical powers cannot blot out her evening smile."

'"To the Lord of heaven the empire is not worth
more than a whirl of dust,
and if the true glory of the world hatched Israel
it happened in the deep night and with hardly a pause.

Follia dels reialmes! N'hi ha de tan balders
que en fa escampall qualsevol nit de maltempsada
i d'altres de tan mínvols que moren als recers
de vall entaforada.
Ningú que mai afronti Sió durarà més
que no pas ella, closa i escampada.
Iahvè, Iahvè! Tot quant vindrà al sentit
és la promesa fina o el rastre esmorteït
d'un Déu, d'un pare igual, Senyor de meravelles.
Istar, com totes elles,
de l'ombra inicial ha eixit
on Ell posà, durant un surt de ses parpelles,
el capciró del dit. —
Mireu si no del bell jardí damunt la flaire! —
Era a l'hora foscant,
i ensems que un gran voltor feia ròdols per l'aire
muntà fins a la dea un núvol rondinaire
i caigué sang del centelleig distant.

Els màgics de la Cort, blancs com el vori
davant el llarg lament que tot el poble féu:
— Gran és Istar, oh rei! — cridaven en desori —.
Podem armar prodigis més bells que els del jueu! —

I sol, ben dret, en aquell pàvid consistori,
el rei manà que els bandegessin de prop seu.
— Ah fatigants oracles
i eixorca veu que dins la pompa mor,
ah mantinguts i encarregats dels espectacles,
ah ben pascuts que només feu miracles
i ja oblidàreu l'alçaprem del cor!
De les mirades que us imploren no sou dignes.
De cada meravella n'haveu tots sols el fruit.
Afalagueu els delirants amb signes,
però, fet d'esma, el signe és buit.

Folly of kingdoms! Some are so shaky
that one stormy night will scatter them,
and others are so feeble that they'll disappear,
tucked away in the fold of remote valleys.
No one confronting Zion will outlast her,
enclosed or dispersed.
Jehovah, Jehovah! All that the senses will gain
are slender promises or blurred traces
of a God, Father of all, Lord of wonders.
Ishtar, like all other stars,
appeared from the initial darkness,
where with the tip of His finger He placed it
in a sudden blinking of His eyes.
Gaze, if you will, above the scented garden!"
It was at the close of day,
as a great vulture circled in the air,
when a grumbling cloud ascended to the goddess,
and from the distant twinkling, blood dropped.

'The court's magicians, ivory-white
in face of the endless lament of the people:
"Great is Ishtar, O King!" they shouted in disarray.
"We can display greater wonders than those of the Jew!"

'And standing erect, a lone figure in the frightened
      assembly,
the king ordered their expulsion from his sight.
"Ah tiresome oracles
of futile voice amid all the pomp unheard,
ah you of easy life in charge of spectacles,
ah well-fed miracle workers
who have long forgotten the power of the heart!
You are not worthy of those who entreat you.
From each marvel you alone benefit.
You flatter the raving crowd with signs,
but a sign given routinely is worthless.

I l'enviat que ens ve no fa semblant de sacre;
era com tots, vivia jup sobre el terrer:
però l'ha pres un Déu que arbora el simulacre
com arborava l'esbarzer.
I és un passant negat que diu paraules pures:
un tast de vi nou ens ha dat
i el pellingot que porta pel cup fou esquitxat;
ens lliura grans de blat
i és ple, damunt son cos, de les garbelladures.
Un gran alè dintre sa veu escombra
en cada temple l'espantall obès;
les ombres que adoràvem ja són al fons de l'ombra
i ens deixen sols amb aquest Déu que ens pren sencers.
Ai de qui el cor no senti fendre's,
ja bestraient el càstig de son mal,
abans que Assur no sigui cendres
i Nínive un sorral! –

    I el rei baixà de son seient de pedreria,
i tombà els ulls que l'averany adoloria.
Als quatre vents tirà sos amulets del coll
i cada auri penjoll
dels costats de sa cara,
i petjà sa tiara;
i per a prosternar-se en nuesa animal,
rebaté son cinyell de gemmes pures,
es va arrencar les brodadures
i migpartí la túnica amb el darrer punyal.

    – He caminat com en follia,
m'han pres com una febre les vanes lluïssors;
i ara bada mos ulls aquest parlar raspós
i entenc de mon irat poder la llebrosia.
I em tornen les tenebres i el pensament amarg
i aquella pietat, que creia d'esma esclava,

And the messenger we have here does not seem holy;
he was like many, living bent over his fields:
but he has been seized by a God that sets the image
    ablaze
as He set ablaze the bush.
And he is a shipwrecked herald who utters pure words:
he has given us a taste of new wine
and the rags he wears are spattered with wine;
he gives us grains of wheat
and his body is covered with coarse siftings.
With majestic voice he sweeps away
from each temple those obese, scary figures;
those shadows we worshipped are now below shadow,
and they leave us alone with this God who takes us whole.
Woe to him who does not feel his heart break
at the impending punishment for his misdeeds,
before Asshur is reduced to ashes
and Nineveh turned into desert sand!"

'And the king descended from his jewel-encrusted seat,
averting his omen-afflicted eyes.
He threw to the four winds his amulets
and the gold earrings
from each side of his face,
and stamped on his tiara;
and in order to prostrate himself in his animal nudity,
he flung away his belt of pure gems,
tore off the embroidered embellishments,
and with the last dagger slashed his tunic.

' "I've been walking as if deranged,
I've surrendered to feverish, idle splendours;
that rasping voice has opened my eyes,
and I understand the leprosy of my irate power.
Dark and bitter thoughts return
and the piety which I thought was enslaved by inertia,

de quan, infant, per primer cop amb el meu arc
vaig aterrar l'ocell que per la llum volava.
Oh Déu, dóna'm consol!
De la ciutat en runes, poblada d'invisibles,
del bosc incendiat, del molí que no mol,
del camp on ja no van del riu les fresques fibles,
de guerra i pau horribles,
sota tos ulls em dol.
Davant tes nacions esquarterades
em vinc a penedir,
de tantes d'esperances violades
i del gemec d'il·lusions mai congriades,
mortes en l'atri del matí;
dels closos i marjades
que ja cap home no veurà florir.

Però més que com rei pecava encara
com servidor d'un temple d'antiguitat preclara
que avui ton Déu trabuca i venç,
car jo posava l'extermini damunt l'ara
i l'he voltat de ciris i volterols d'encens.
«Occiu», vaig dir, «fins les no nades criatures:
els déus ho troben falaguer.
La rialla davant de les tortures
farà saltar llurs ventres de plaer».

Car una nit estranya del fons de les centúries,
en la misteriosa derrota dels humans,
finaren en la terra les càndides cantúries
i els àngels no vingueren a seure-hi com abans.
I els homes en la cova, fumats amb l'aspra teia,
el fort lleó temeren i el sinuós volpell;
a animal brut servia tot home, i estrafeia
sos crits, i es prosternava per caminar com ell.

as when, in my childhood, for the first time with my bow
I brought down the bird that flew through the light.
O God, comfort me!
I grieve for the city in ruins, peopled by ghosts,
for the burnt-out woods, for the mill which does not
    grind,
for the land where fresh downpours do not find rivers,
for war and horrific peace
under your gaze.
Before your dismembered nations
I come to repent,
for so many violated hopes,
for the groan of dreams never realized,
dead at morning's gate;
for hedges and meadows
that no man will see blossoming.

'"But more than as king, I've sinned
as servant of an ancient and renowned temple
which today your God conquers and overturns,
for I had placed extermination on the altar stone,
and surrounded it with candles and whiffs of incense.
'Kill,' I said, 'down to the unborn child:
it is gratifying to the gods.
Their laughter witnessing the tortures
will make their bellies jump with joy.'

'"Because of a remarkable night centuries ago,
when humanity suffered a mysterious defeat,
innocent songs were silenced on earth
and angels ceased to descend as before.
And men in caves, blackened with torch smoke,
feared the mighty lion and the furtive fox;
and the human species aped the brute animal, imitating
their cries, walking on four legs.

Després, el seny cercava la llum: el déu ja fóra
o força o traidoria, i l'animal, altar.
Hom volgué fer-se estada del déu, enganyadora;
i disfressats de monstres els homes van dansar.
I un jorn deien a l'ídol: «Molt d'honrament usurpes:
car ja som forts pel glavi i el seny enganyador».
I els ídols foren homes duent els corns, les urpes,
amb potes cavallines o ales de falcó.
I l'esperit, en créixer, menà damunt les ares
l'enter caient de l'home amb els més bells arreus,
i hom proclamà divines les pietats més clares
i els darrers déus tenien un animal als peus.
I jo, servent del temple, i havent de fer més nobles
els déus, contrast de l'home que cau i vol i dol,
he dat al drac innúmer per víctimes els pobles
i he retornat els temples al primitiu udol.

Però, tantost, la roba de sac duré cenyida
i m'asseuré en la cendra miseriosament.
Oh mos heralds, feu crida
per tota la ciutat del gran penediment!
Ordre del rei i de sos pros vinguda:
«Ni l'home, ni l'animal servidor,
arment, cabra o moltó,
no tastarà cap més menjar, cap més beguda;
hom vestirà roba de sac
i es colgarà en la cendra;
i cadascú, retent a Déu el cor manyac,
bandejarà aquell mal que estava a punt d'emprendre».
Iahvè féu pacte amb el nafrat i amb el mesquí,
i al desdonat es gira.

Later, the mind searched for light: the god would become
either a force or a deceit, and the beast an altar.
Man tried to accept the god, wrongly;
and dressed like monsters they danced.
And one day they said to the idol: 'You are an usurper
    of honours:
we have become strong by the sword and through
    beguiling wisdom.'
And the idols were men with horns, claws,
hooves or falcon's wings.
And the spirit, as it gained force, brought to the altar
    stone
the whole of man's appearance dressed in finery,
and declared divine the most obvious piety,
and the last gods had a beast at their feet.
And I, servant of the temple, and wanting to ennoble
the gods, in contrast to the man who falls and wants
    and grieves,
I've sacrificed peoples to many a dragon
and I gave back the temples to the primitive howl.

' "But as soon as I girdle the sackcloth
and sit down wretchedly on ashes,
I'll summon my heralds to cry
all over the town the great repentance!
This order comes from the king and his elders:
'Let neither man nor household animal,
livestock, goat or lamb,
be fed or watered;
let everybody be dressed in sackcloth
and cover himself with ashes;
and each one, raising his humble heart to God,
will reject the evil he was about to commit.'
Jehovah made peace with the infirm and the wretched,
and turns towards the unprovided.

¿Qui sap si un plor d'amor faria decandir
la foguerada de sa ira? —

I el rei i el poble en pietat i por sagrada,
de la desesperança i el dol en l'entreforc,
escolliren el dol, ple d'estelada —
l'ànima en Déu apaivagada
com doll de torrentera que va esplaiant-se al gorg.

Who knows if a cry of love would abate
the blaze of His wrath?"

'And the king and his people, in piety and sacred awe,
between grief and helplessness,
chose a starlit grief:
soothed by God, the soul was like
a gully stream flowing contentedly into a deep pool.'

VIII

I el dia terç, en veure sota la posta d'or
aquella cleda penedida
que bandejava l'urc, la mala vida
i l'eixutor de cor,
apaivagà Iahvè les celles,
deixà el braç amollit sobre el genoll
i deturà a sos peus les negres meravelles
que tot quant viu s'emmenen, com la ventada el boll.

Idols bicornes o d'escata agafatosa
atònits badallaven en sòcols oblidats;
armes, joiells damunt la cendra eren bolcats,
com esperant del foc de Déu una altra fosa.
En la dissort, que unia planyents de tota mena,
una bagassa vella del port, del rei la pena
apaivagava amb compassat bruel.
I a un màgic que tenia de fems la barba plena,
deia un infant: — Oh, mira enlaire! Amb la serena
baixa el perdó del cel —.

Llavors amb una cremorada
de mortificació
vaig dir: — ¿Per què t'has compadit altra vegada,
Iahvè, que encara portes l'inic en ta abraçada,
aviciat com un nadó?
Ta veu que m'estordeix i que m'arbora
he seguit amb mil minves de deler,
amb cama de tolit, ranquejadora . . .
i jo sabia prou per què.

Car el dit que en deixant el vell Noè sa barca
pintava l'iris sobre el núvol fonedís

VIII

'And on the third day, seeing underneath the golden
    sunset
such a penitent fold
rejecting arrogance, corrupt life
and dryness of heart,
Jehovah softened His brow,
let His tender arm rest on His knee,
and stopped at His feet the dark wonders
that in all living things are like chaff in a gust of wind.

'Idols, bicorned or with tacky scales,
yawned astounded on forgotten pedestals;
arms and jewels were discarded over ashes,
as though waiting for God's fire for a new fusion.
In the distress uniting the doleful and varied crowd,
an old harbour whore moaning monotonously
soothed the king's sorrow.
And to a magician with a dung-dirtied beard,
a child said: "Oh, look overhead! With the dew
heaven's forgiveness comes down."

'Then in a fierce burst
of mortification
I said: "Why have You again shown compassion,
Jehovah, embracing the wicked
as You would embrace a new-born?
With faltering eagerness
I've followed Your voice which stuns and inflames me,
trailing my leg like a cripple . . .
and I well knew why.

'"Because the finger which painted the rainbow
on the disappearing cloud when old Noah left the Ark

és el que assenyalà Caín amb una marca
perquè cap home no l'occís.
Com que em temia que series tendre,
vela a Tartessos vaig curar de prendre;
cal que et traeixin segles per a dar-te l'afany de maleir
i encara te'n desdius a mig camí.
Qui vols que em cregui ara,
si corre a plaer seu qui havies encalçat!
Jo he sentit que em parlaves cara a cara
i avui te m'has girat —.

I quan creguí que des del blau palau
Iahvè tot endeuat s'abocaria a posta,
mon cor es va estremir de l'íntima resposta:
— ¿És que l'ira t'escau? —
Com l'infant engrunyit que es desatansa
del mot suau,
vaig partir de l'indret de ma recança
per un camí sense aigua ni cap ombratge verd,
el de la penitència i la desesperança,
car totes dues menen al desert.

I a l'endemà, i a l'hora lleu que brolla
la claredat del món, en un indret
tot solitari i tot lluent de set
on no hi hagué jamai fil d'aigua ni cadolla,
recomençà a pleret
de rondinar ma boca folla.

— Tu em deies: «¿Què en fareu de l'arc i de la fona?
Que els lliuri en presentalla la vostra pura fe,
car no dureu sinó una estona
i jo só qui roman, Iahvè.
No cap enginy de guerra valdria l'esperança

is the same one that marked Cain with a sign,
lest anyone finding him should kill him.
As I feared that You would be soft-hearted,
I sought to set sail towards Tarshish;
You have to be betrayed for centuries before You are
    roused to curse,
and even then You falter halfway.
Who is going to believe me now
if You let run free those whom You have pursued!
I felt that You were talking to me face to face,
and today You turn away from me."

'And when I thought that from the blue mansion
Jehovah, indebted, would lean over designedly,
my heart trembled at the answer within me:
"Does wrath befit You?"
Like the bad-tempered child scorning
a gentle word,
I left the place of my vexation
by a waterless and shadowless path,
that of penitence and forlorn hope,
for both lead to the desert.

'And next day, when the world's soft hour
of daylight appears, in a desolate spot
shining with thirst,
which has never seen a trickle of water nor a pond,
my demented mouth
slowly started to mutter.

'Then You said: "What will you do with a bow and
    a sling?
Let your pure faith offer them up to Me,
for you last but a while
and I, Jehovah, am the one that remains.
No war device would be worth the hope

en Qui senyal no deixa de brolla o renadiu.
Encomaneu-me la venjança;
quan Iahvè passa, res no viu.
A l'ase fer, que corre a la perduda,
daré el palau del rei, clofolla d'or rompuda;
a l'òliba, la torre que els núvols ajaçà.
El tron impur, el sangonós altar,
un torterol de fum seran a nit vinguda
i un torterol de sorra els colgarà».
Deies així i el món temia tos temperis.
Potser ja els emissaris alats de tos misteris,
ans de complir del càstig el manament incert,
es giren vers tos ulls per si l'enuig s'hi perd;
potser ja massa glòria colgada té el desert,
aquest cementiri d'imperis –.

I en l'àrid lloc
vaig adormir-me sota un sol de foc;
després, amb la parpella encar no ben desclosa,
vaig veure que una planta hi havia al meu costat,
una de branc tot argentat
que al bat del sol oposa
un cobricel d'estels de verda fosquedat,
cada un gronxat
dalt d'una tija rosa.

Goig del món, el branc i les fulles!
Donen casa a tothom que va i ve;
paren jaç les verdes despulles
mentre les fulles vives el somni fan lleuger.
I Déu hi parla amb veu gentil i reverenda;
els ulls hi troben joia i el pensament la pau.
Branc i fulles, miracle suau,
valen més que els pals de la tenda,
valen més que els pals de la nau.

in Him who leaves no sign of undergrowth or rebirth.
Entrust vengeance to Me;
when Jehovah passes, nothing lives.
To the ass running wild I'll give
the king's palace, a broken golden shell;
to the owl the tower laid out by the clouds.
The impure throne, the blood-stained altar,
will become at night whirling smoke
and swirling sands will cover them up."
Thus You spoke, and the world was in fear of Your wrath.
Perhaps the winged emissaries of Your mysteries,
before carrying out the punishment of Your doubtful
    command,
will search Your eyes for signs of compassion;
perhaps the desert, that grave of empires,
has enough buried glory.

'And in that arid place
I slept under a burning sun;
later, my eyelids hardly open,
I saw next to me a plant
with silvery branches
which in the glaring sun
offered me a dark green stellar canopy,
each star swinging
from a rose-coloured stem.

'Leaves and branches, joy of the world!
They give shelter to each and all;
the fallen leaves offer a resting-place,
while the living leaves induce peaceful dreams.
And God speaks there with gentle and reverent voice;
a joy to the eyes, peace to the mind.
Leaves and branches, gentle miracle,
worth more than the tent's poles,
worth more than the ship's masts.

Cap angoixa mon cor no destria
sota aquest murmuri disert.
¿Quin delirós ha pensat mai que trobaria
la primavera en el desert?

Vaig viure un dia a l'ombra regalada;
i a l'endemà al matí,
a trenc d'albada,
Déu, que la planta havia fet ahir,
envià el verm que amb son rosec la consumí.
I Déu encara féu venir un xaloc
d'ales de pols, de sorra i foc,
fúria de l'infern donant-se festa
que a giravolts guspirejà,
talment irada contra tot demà.

I jo deia a sacsades:
— Val més morir que no pas viure. Mort,
vine, et rebria a mans besades;
vull el teu palmell per suport.
Oh Mort, porta final i cúpula complida,
honorat desament de l'humà desencís,
oh tu que els viatgers aculls amb l'ombradís,
oh lloc sense consol i, almenys, sense partida! —

Una veu deturà ma complanta:
Iahvè parlant com a un petit que hagués pres mal.
— ¿És que per una planta
l'ira t'escau? — Cert, una ira mortal.
— Et dol un poc de brosta; i no passares pena
a fer-ho néixer ni ho pujares tu;
fou un present de la serena
i una rosada matinal se n'ho va dur.
I a mi, que faig i peixo totes les coses nades,
¿no ha de recar-me gens
Nínive, la ciutat de tres jornades,

My heart remains untroubled
under such eloquent murmur.
Would anyone in his wildest dreams have imagined
springtime in the desert?

'I lived for a day under the pleasurable shade,
and the following morning,
at the break of dawn,
God, who had made the plant the day before,
sent a worm which gnawing consumed it.
And God also sent a south-easterly wind
with wings of dust, sand and fire,
hell's fury in a display
of sparkling whirls,
in His rage against all time to come.

'And shaking I mumbled:
"Better to die than to live. Death,
come, I'll welcome you with open arms;
I need the palm of your hand to support me.
O Death, the last gate and final dome,
honoured laying to rest of the human disenchantment!
O you, giver of a welcoming shadow to the traveller!
O comfortless spot with no way out."

'A voice halted my lamentation:
Jehovah speaking as though to a hurt child.
"Does a plant
befit your anger?" "True, a mortal anger."
"You grieve for a little foliage; yet you had
no part in planting it or making it grow;
it was a gift of the night air,
and a morning dew took it away.
And to Me, who makes and tends all born things,
should not Nineveh, the three days' city, concern Me;

amb cent vint mil infants, malconeixents
d'on tenen la mà esquerra i la mà dreta,
i amb tanta de gran pleta
i el devessall d'arments? —

I en cessant Iahvè jo capia
que Ell no havia parlat des d'un ròdol tot clar
del cel, sinó de dins de mi, que l'ofenia.
En el nostre esperit, on ningú no el destria,
al dellà de cent cambres Déu nia;
i l'home de sa casa s'ajeu en el llindar
com un servent, com un ca.

a city with a hundred and twenty thousand children
    ignorant
of which is their left or right hand,
and with numberless sheep-pens
and great herds of cattle?"

'And as Jehovah finished I realized
that He had not spoken from a clear patch of sky,
but from within myself who had offended Him.
In our soul, where no one perceives Him,
God lives in over a hundred chambers;
and man lies on the threshold of His house
like a servant, like a dog.'

IX

En el son, una nit, vaig deixar mon trespol.

A una llum verda i poca,
– Que lluny no sóc! – em deia, mirant tot las al volt.
Cames penjant damunt la roca,
em creia d'ésser-hi tot sol.
I en cavil·lar per quin lloc tiraria,
i en decantant les vores d'abriülls
l'últim sospir del dia,
de sobte, més que no veia, sentia
d'algú, darrera meu, els ulls.
Afectada de grec digué una veu: – T'enterques,
amic, rodant de destret en destret,
escarnit en cada poblet
on dius que t'ha parlat el déu que encara cerques! –
Ell modulava cantarella molt civil,
amb la parpella migcloent-se, compadida:
l'aire que feia aquella veu subtil
em gelava la nuca ajupida.

(Quan Déu sospesa
un cor i diu: – Serà mon confident –,
a poc a poc el desavesa
d'enraonies amb la gent.
Qui Déu escolta de tot es destria,
qui Déu escolta l'alè té nuat,
qui Déu contempla, l'herbei damunt seu creixeria,
qui Déu contempla fa cara d'orat;
i si caigués, d'Ell encara encisat,
entraria en la mort per la porta del dia.
I l'home fet feréstec per l'alta solitud,

IX

'One night, in my dreams, I left home.

'The light was green and diffused.
"I'm so far away!" I said to myself, as wearily I looked
    around.
With legs hanging free from a rock
I believed myself to be all alone.
While I was considering which road I would take,
and the last breath of the day
was bending a bank of thistles,
all of a sudden, more than seeing them, I felt
somebody's eyes on my back.
With an affected Greek accent a voice said: "Friend,
you are indeed obstinate, roaming from trouble to
    trouble,
being mocked in every village where you
proclaim that the god you are seeking spoke to you!"
This was uttered in a very civil sing-song voice,
with eyelids half-closed, in compassion:
the air from that gentle sound
was freezing the nape of my stooping neck.

'(When God estimates the value
of a heart, and says: "It will be my confidant",
He gradually disengages it
from idle talk with people.
Whosoever listens to God disavows all,
whosoever listens to God chokes,
whosoever contemplates God, grass will grow over him,
whosoever contemplates God looks demented;
and should he fall, still under His spell,
he would approach death through the gate of day.
And man, grown wild from the aloofness on high,

dels afalacs no té consuetud
i no li plau qui, esbraveït, fa com donzella
i parla amb capcineig i cantarella;
qui ha esdevingut esquerp no es fia de qui brella,
i veu senyal d'insídies dels genis traïdors
en l'home obsequiós.)

   — ¿Qui en terra tan immemorada i sola
— pensava jo — manyagament m'acull? —
Sota la nit que enfosqueïa la rossola
jo sols guaitava enrera, de reüll.
— És tot el que veiem — sentia — polseguera;
de miques frisadores és l'alta roquetera,
els arbres, vós i jo i el sauló del camí.
Tot mor i torna i roda sense fi;
i si enllà de la trèmula rodera
hi hagués algú diví,
bell punt mirés, ple de l'afany de la carrera,
vindria al remolí.
Res no pot eximir-se del destí
de moure's si no és curant de no existir.
— Ta parla que m'alerta — jo deia — no em trastoca,
oh tu, sobrevingut quan a ponent
moria l'últim encenall ardent,
tu que et torces al volt de la soca
com si estrafessis el serpent,
i d'ulls encesos en la nit com la miloca.
Qui sota el mal encís
el nom de Déu rebolca en l'ira,
encara es té, valent pel seu permís,
en l'alè d'aire que imprecant respira;
qui nega Déu
no nega més que un sòrdid pensar que ell sol es féu;
qui vol eixir-se'n hi ensopega;

will spurn customary flattery
and will dislike the faint-hearted who behaves like
    a maiden
and speaks head-wobbling in a chanting voice;
a mistrustful person does not fall easily into a set trap,
and sees in the obsequious man
the crafty mark of treacherous spirits.)

' "Who is it that in such a forgotten and deserted land,"
I thought, "greets me with honeyed words?"
Beneath the night-darkened slippery slope
I was looking askance behind me.
"All that we see," I heard, "is endless dust;
the rocky face above is made of restless stones,
the trees, you and I, and the gravelled path.
Everything dies and returns and revolves without end;
and if beyond the tremulous sunken ruts
someone divine existed,
on first sight, in the impetus of the journey,
he would be drawn into the whirlwind.
No one can be free from his predestined
wandering unless he tries not to exist."
"Your words are a warning," I said, "but I'm unmoved,
O you, who came into being when
the last burning fire died in the West,
spiralling yourself round the tree-trunk
mimicking the serpent,
with eyes glowing at night like the owl.
Whosoever under an evil spell
spurns in anger God's name,
still needs His permission
for the breath of air that, cursing, he breathes;
whosoever denies God
denies simply the sordid idea he himself has conceived;
whosoever wants to escape Him stumbles;

el trist i abandonat el fa venir quan prega;
dins son esclat es tapa d'ulls el fugitiu
i qui l'ignora en viu —.

    Amb veu que tot amanyagant s'arrisca
ell responia a mon roent parlar:
era la cura pèrfida que llisca
per a malmetre i entortolligar.
— Tinc gran dubtança
que sigui qui tant és i tan opac s'atansa.
Mentre jo visc, vejam, ¿què fa?
No en tinc esment ni en sé les noves.
No hi val recórrer els cims, entrar a les coves.
Si viu, aquí té un cingle: que em faci rodolar —.

    Vaig fer-me enrera,
d'esglai del Déu ofès.
I vaig mirar: ningú per l'alta roquetera,
i al mig del cel no res.
I en la nit buida que tots sons aplaca,
més buida per l'absència del llamp responedor,
emplenà mes orelles la ressaca
de la meva maror.

    I va esclatar la riallada
del descreient;
i tot seguit em va muntar la foguerada
d'un pensament:
— La teva fe salva amatent! —
I amb un escreix de força fera
vaig anar al reptador com un esperitat,
i aferrant-lo pel pit ben anusat
el vaig capitombar per la cinglera.

the unhappy and the forlorn seek Him when praying;
dazzled, the fugitive covers his eyes,
and whosoever ignores Him lives by Him."

'In an unguarded, caressing voice
he answered my ardent words:
it was a treacherous concern which glides
to hurt and to entwine.
"I greatly doubt the existence
of one so powerful yet so obscure in His coming.
While I live, let's see, what is He doing?
I'm not aware of Him nor do I have news of Him.
There's no point in traversing mountain peaks,
        penetrating caves.
If He exists, here is a steep rock: let Him throw me over."

'I recoiled
in terror at God offended.
I looked around: nobody on the high cliff,
and in the sky, nothing.
In the emptiness of a night damping all sound,
made more empty by the absence of echoing lightning,
a swirling tide of agitation
flooded my ears.

'And the unbeliever
burst out laughing;
and suddenly a thought
flared up in me:
"I'll have to save my faith now!"
And in a wild fury, as if possessed,
I threw myself at the challenger,
and clutching his sinewy chest
I flung him head-first down the cliff.

I en reculant-ne d'esma, un cop atroç
cuidava fer-me caure tot flac, sense homenia;
i era només un so que m'estordia:
la batzegada, en un relleix, del cos.

D'uns panicals arrapissaire
em vaig tenir, desfet, en un esquei de l'erm.
M'amenaçà el penyal, em féu vergonya l'aire.
Déu em deixava del fondal al caire
arraulit com un verm.

I clarament, com una música sentia:
— Cap flastomia
com negar que Déu és perdó.
Car Abel fou son servidor.
I si Déu fos malsofridor,
¿qui mai viuria?
¿Qui diu: «Jo venjo Déu»? ¿Qui s'aparella
a menar Déu contra fantasmes fugitius?
Ell abraça el llop i l'ovella
i l'esparver i els nius.
Ell és qui esbrolla la garriga
i esporgarà son bell verger, faixat de rius.
Li lleva senyoria qui castiga;
per a la vida ens aixecà
i ens la prendrà quan l'hora siga:
així com a l'infant que veu el món minvar
perquè sos ulls s'acluquen de fadiga,
hom pren una parença de cosa amb què jugà —.

Llavors, negat al fons de més gran fondalada
que no l'occit, el cap alçava com
si no gosés; i en veure escrita en l'estelada
una promesa per pietat traspuntada,
a rossegons per terra vaig adorar son Nom.

'And as I drew back instinctively, a dreadful blow
knocked me senseless;
it was only a sound that stunned me:
the impact of the body on a ledge.

'Clinging onto a spiky plant I found
myself, despairing, in a fissure of the wilderness.
The cliff was menacing me, the air filled me with shame.
God left me at the edge of the abyss,
curled up like a worm.

'And clearly, like music, I heard:
"There is no greater blasphemy
than denying that God is forgiveness.
For Abel was his servant.
And if God were not forbearing,
who would ever live?
Who says: 'I avenge God'?
Who enlists God against runaway phantoms?
He embraces the wolf and the lamb,
the hawk and the brood.
It is He who clears the scrub
and trims His beautiful rivers-enriched orchard.
Whosoever punishes diminishes His lordship;
He raised us to life,
and He'll take it back when the time comes;
as with a child who sees the world shrinking
when his eyes close with tiredness,
one appears to have been a toy in His hands."

'Then, as though drowned in a deeper gully
than my victim, hesitantly I raised my head,
and on seeing written in the starry sky
a clear promise of compassion,
crawling I worshipped His name.'

X

El Líban era en el tombant de l'any
que del xacal s'acosta a l'home el plany,
i els núvols s'agarbonen al cel i el vent somica.
Ja la cigala amb la seva musica
no serrava la soca del pi;
hi havia arrossegalls de boira pel camí;
anava a jóc més aviat la tarda;
l'última flor, la flor de l'olivarda,
veia un cel fet de fredolic setí.

Jonàs, que en la blancor de sa vellesa
bleixava sense dubte ni corcó,
mirava la tendresa
del cel, darrera el curt afany d'un ploviscó,
i es llevava, per seure, la capçana
i el cove amb pa i amb herbes, en el flanc
d'un dolç turó que veu la mar llunyana
i que els ceps filetegen com de sang.

— Al repòs sota còdols i pinassa
— deia Jonàs — va decantant-se el cos:
he caminat i caminat lluny de mon tros,
i ja a una balma estreta en mi tot es compassa:
mos ulls s'escurcen, mon alè i ma passa,
mon front s'ajup, com demanant repòs.
«Si jo sol no morís!», el foll medita.
En el primer jardí, però, la llei fou dita:
«Véns de la pols i te n'hi vas»;
«Hi tornaràs», diu l'home, «per no tornar-ne pas».

X

It was towards the end of the year in Lebanon,
when the cry of the jackal draws near to man,
and clouds cluster in the sky and the wind whines softly.
The chirping cicada no longer
frets the pine tree trunk;
flocks of mist float over the road;
the evening sinks earlier;
the last flower, the flower of the elecampane,
gazes upon a cool satin sky.

Jonah, who in the whiteness of his old age
breathed once more free of gnawing doubts,
contemplated the tenderness
of the sky after a short, soft rain,
and rose to take his mat and basket
filled with bread and herbs, to sit on the flank
of a pleasant hill overlooking the distant sea
bordered by vineyards which seemed to drip blood.

'To lie down,' Jonah said, 'among pebbles
and pine needles is what my body seeks;
I've walked and walked far from my plot,
and now in a narrow recess of my being all is harmony;
my sight shortens, my breath and my steps languish,
my head nods, as though asking for repose.
"If I were the only one not to die!" the fool ponders.
In the original garden, though, the law had been
    pronounced:
"You come from dust and you'll become dust."
"You'll go towards it," man says, "without possible
    return."

La terra que et portava enorgullida,
Adam, hereu del món, mai no t'oblida;
feixugues les centúries li féu semblar ton son,
i té por del secret de ta dormida
que t'envileix i et descompon.
I mentre cada gènera esgota fugidora
els seus matins vermells,
la terra encara enyora
el sol en tos cabells.
I encara fores com un arbre que s'enfila
si hagués pogut la terra bestreure ton rescat,
pols de la pols de la primera argila
que ens encomanes la caducitat.

I anem a tu en rengleres,
Adam, darrera teu, pel camí vell.
Ni podem veure aqueixa llum que tant volgueres
sense pensar que emmanllevem el seu mantell.
I tanmateix, ton espirall de glòria
es reflectí dels éssers en l'eixam.
Breu com la nostra nit, és transitòria
la teva nit sota segell, Adam.
Canteu del comiat en l'hora amarga
el cant de bres més dolç.
Car Déu tothora crea i l'univers allarga,
i de la mort farà brillar la pols.
Oh primogènit dels vivents, colgat un dia
per l'àngel, dins la cova que només ell sabia,
d'una complanta de la terra als greus acords:
un Fill teu s'alçarà del penyal on dormia
sense cap senyal de dissorts,
no pas desfet en pols i cendra,
d'alba encerclat per on la mort el volgué prendre
i primer nat dels morts.
Perquè Déu lleva
només vivents i desconeix la llei mortal;

'Adam, the world's heir, the earth that proudly
carried you, never forgets you;
your sleep made the centuries seem oppressive,
and fears the secret of your dream
which degrades and disembodies you.
And while each fleeting generation
dissipates its vermilion morns,
the earth still longs for
the sun on your hair.
And you could still be like a tree reaching for the sky
if the earth had paid your ransom,
dust of dust of the original clay
that transmits to us caducity.

'And we go in file, Adam, behind you,
following the ancient path.
And we cannot see that light so dear to you
without thinking that we are borrowing its mantle.
And clearly your shaft of glory
is reflected itself in great numbers of human beings.
Adam, your transient night under seal
is as short as our own.
In the farewell of the bitter hour we sing
the sweetest of cradle-songs.
For God ever creates and expands the universe
and He will make death's dust glitter.
O primogenitor of the living, once buried
by an angel inside a cave known only to himself,
accompanied by earth's sombre harmony:
with no sign of misfortune a Son of yours
will rise, first-born from the dead,
from the stone where he slept,
not as dust and ashes, but encircled
by dawn from where death had wanted to take Him.
Because God takes
only the living and ignores mortal law;

ni per a pols ni ossos no va donar la seva
aliança eternal.
I contra l'acaballa tenim una promesa
de Déu, a cada gènera represa,
més alta en Abraham que no pas en Noè.
És fent presents com Déu augmenta sa riquesa,
Ell sa promesa eixampla més que el vivent sa fe.

El primogènit nou dirà, del cel gaubança:
«Tot ço que té Déu em pertany».
I Ell, que veurà que a son voler s'atansa
la volior dels àngels fins a la vall de plany,
dia vindrà que amb gent al volt aplegadissa,
sospiri, las de llur demanadissa:
«Oh conradors de pobres pedregars,
oh pescadors de xarxa vella!
Ans no passeu del món, hi haurà una meravella:
jo us donaré el miracle de Jonàs».
Car Ell, per conhortar les nostres agonies
i ungir-nos en la pau dels averanys complerts,
dins de la gola de la mort viurà tres dies,
alliberat el dia terç.
I pel solc argentat de ses passes serenes,
serà trobat més bell, en paga de ses penes,
per entenents d'amor el paradís,
sempre més lluny de les cruels carenes
i el vell altar sagnant damunt l'abís.
Descorregut com un tapís,
el cel a la nissaga redimida
descobrirà la fi de les edats.
L'arbre i el roc que gemen resplendiran de vida
en veure els sants glorificats.
La mort serà vençuda en sos estatges
i esdevindran herois les cendres que consum

it was not for dust and bones that He gave
His eternal alliance.
And against our dying days we have
God's promise, renewed with each generation,
stronger for Abraham than for Noah.
It is by His gifts that God becomes richer,
He extends His promise more than man his faith.

'The New-born, joy of heaven, will say:
"All that God possesses belongs to me."
And for Him, who will see at His command winged
    angels
advancing towards the vale of tears,
the day will come when, with a crowd assembled
    around,
He will sigh, weary of their clamour:
"O tillers of the stony ground,
O fishermen with worn-out nets!
[Before you leave this world, there'll be a marvel:]
I'll give you the miracle of Jonah."
For He, in order to assuage our agonies
and anoint us in the peace of fulfilled prophecies,
inside the gullet of death will live for three days,
freed on the third day.
And along His serene silvery tracks,
Paradise, ever further from the cruel ridges
and the ancient altar bleeding over the abyss,
through love understood will be found more beautiful,
as a reward for His pains.
Drawn back like a tapestry,
heaven will disclose to the redeemed race
the end of all ages.
The moaning tree and rock will burst into life
on seeing the saints glorified.
Death will be defeated in its lair,
and the consuming ashes will become heroes,

i la sang renaixent es farà llum
i el cos serà venjat de sos ultratges –.

Així Jonàs parlava a l'hora que es desmaia
el dia, i el silenci s'allarga per l'afrau,
i el cor, feixuc de cansaments, s'esplaia
en un sospir de pau;
l'enraonia del fullatge plega;
pel tomb del cel una tendror s'escau;
manyac un núvol s'esllenega,
esborrant ell mateix son blanc palau;
i en qui s'adiu a la dolçor nocturna,
un pensament de pietat llampurna
com un estel que cau.

– Salta en mon cor com un infant al raig del dia,
oh pensament de Déu,
tu que ajustes els plecs de l'alegria
i fas com amb un cant el nostre dol més breu.
Oh jaç, oh font que corre, oh tast de marinada,
ull d'or mirant per les escletxes del parral,
i, a l'hora que estavella la calda empolsegada,
ombra segura d'un penyal.
Car tota cosa, tret de Déu, és fugissera.
¿Qui dirà mai ses menes d'eternes resplendors
en parla forastera
i amb llavi farfallós?
Adéu, però, grans grapes de càstig i avarícia!
Morir per a la nova naixó, clara delícia!
Només amor esdevindrà l'home rebel.
Car ultrapassaràs del Pare la justícia,
oh maternal condícia
del brossat, de les pomes i la mel!

and the reborn blood will become light,
and the body will be avenged for its ravages.'

Thus Jonah spoke at the hour when day
swoons, and silence spreads through the ravine,
and the weary heart expands
with a sigh of peace;
the rustling of the foliage stops;
a tenderness stirs in the sky;
a gentle cloud stretches out,
wiping clear its own white mansion;
and in whosoever is at one with the sweetness of night,
a thought of mercy will scintillate
like a falling star.

'O idea of God, leaping in my heart
like an infant's at the light of day,
You who arrange the folds of joy
and with a song shorten our grief.
O repose, O running fountain, O taste of sea-breeze!,
golden eye that sees through the vine's trellis
and, at the hour when the dusty oppressive heat
    blazes down,
the secure shade of a rock.
For, excepting God, all is transient.
Who would ever speak of his own eternal radiances
in a foreign tongue
and with stuttering lips?
Farewell, though, to clawing punishment and avarice!
To die to be born again, clear delight!
The rebellious man will become love itself.
For you'll exceed the justice of the Father,
O maternal purity
of curd, apples and honey!'

Some European poetry in translation from Anvil

Dante: *The Divine Comedy*
Translated by Peter Dale

Nikos Gatsos
Amorgos
Translated by Sally Purcell

Goethe: *Roman Elegies*
and other poems
Translated by Michael Hamburger

Luis de Góngora
Selected Shorter Poems
Translated by Michael Smith

Nikolay Gumilyov
The Pillar of Fire
Translated by Richard McKane

Poems of Jules Laforgue
Translated by Peter Dale

Ivan V. Lalić
A Rusty Needle
Fading Contact
Translated by Francis R Jones

Federico García Lorca
A Season in Granada
Edited and translated by Christopher Maurer

Vasko Popa
Collected Poems
Translated by Anne Pennington and Francis R Jones

Arthur Rimbaud: *A Season in Hell*
and other poems
Translated by Norman Cameron

Poems of François Villon
Translated by Peter Dale